THE OTHER SIDE OF
MIDNIGHT:
TAXICAB STORIES

© 2012, Mike Heffernan

We gratefully acknowledge the financial support of the Canada Council for the Arts, the Government of Canada through the Canada Book Fund (CBF), and the Government of Newfoundland and Labrador through the Department of Tourism, Culture and Recreation for our publishing program.

Cover Design by Darren Whalen
Layout by Todd Manning and Amy Fitzpatrick
Printed on acid-free paper

Published by
CREATIVE PUBLISHERS
an imprint of CREATIVE BOOK PUBLISHING
a Transcontinental Inc. associated company
P.O. Box 8660, Stn. A
St. John's, Newfoundland and Labrador A1B 3T7

Printed in Canada by:
TRANSCONTINENTAL INC.

Heffernan, Mike, 1978-
    The other side of midnight : taxicab stories / Mike Heffernan.

ISBN 978-1-897174-96-8

1. Taxicab drivers--Newfoundland and Labrador--St. John's.
2. Taxicab drivers--Newfoundland and Labrador--St. John's--
Social conditions. 3. Taxicab industry--Newfoundland and Labrador--
St. John's. I. Title.

HD8039.T162C3 2012   388.4'13214097181   C2012-904660-4

THE OTHER SIDE OF
MIDNIGHT:
TAXICAB STORIES

CREATIVE PUBLISHERS

St. John's, Newfoundland and Labrador
2012

For Lesley.

And the taxicab drivers of St. John's.

"Work, is, by its very nature, about violence—to the spirit as well as to the body. It is about ulcers as well as accidents, about shouting matches as well as fistfights, about nervous breakdowns as well as kicking the dog around. It is, above all (or beneath all), about daily humiliations. To survive the day is triumph enough for the walking wounded among the great many of us."

– **Studs Terkel, *Working***

"I taxied up and down this town since 1954
Wore out ten or a dozen cars over thirty years or more
Drove the other side of midnight to the clear edge of dawn
Heard a whole lot of wasn't right
And more of what was wrong."

– **Ron Hynes, "Killer Cab" from *Face to the Gale***

Table of Contents

THE CITY'S TEEMING ENTRAILS ▪▪▪▪▪▪▪▪▪▪▪▪▪▪▪

HACKED TO DEATH

EPILOGUE

Introduction

A Hard Way of Life

"A taxi driver has a way of life. Someone who drives taxi has an occupation. One is a subculture; the other is a job."
– unpublished diary;
quoted in Kimberly Berry, *The Last Cowboy*

The first horse-drawn taxis in St. John's appeared on Water Street in the 1860s. By the start of the First World War, automobiles operating as taxicabs arrived in the city. The industry then went through a boom during the Second World War to accommodate the influx of thousands of Allied (American, British and Canadian) troops. There are now 364 taxis and anywhere from 500 to 1,000 full and part-time taxi drivers operating in St. John's. Exact numbers are difficult to determine because the city only keeps a record of taxicab licence holders. But, outside of the stereotypes, the public doesn't know much about the working lives of taxicab drivers. Even taxi drivers in cities like New York, where they number somewhere in the neighborhood of 40,000, have had surprisingly few serious studies devoted to them.

The Other Side of Midnight: Taxicab Stories is not a traditional history of the St. John's taxicab industry. Instead, it's a collection of first-person monologues based on approximately forty interviews conducted with taxicab drivers and dispatchers over the course of more than three years. Incorporating elements of creative non-fiction and oral history, it describes the commonly shared experiences of an underrecorded portion of Newfoundland's working class.

This book explores the daily experiences of its subjects, as well as their thoughts and feelings about their choice of career and their clients. Every segment of our society, from the elite to the marginal, utilizes their services: business executives, drug pushers, tourists and prostitutes. Comical, absurd and often dramatic, their reminiscences are of long hours and years on the job, high hopes and decayed dreams.

Many St. John's taxi drivers have been working behind the wheel for decades. They have witnessed the city evolve from relative poverty and isolation to the post-1990s financial upswing and the "boomtown" phenomenon that a great deal of of them believe has followed closely on its heels. But it's important to read these monologues within their proper context. As historian Jean Barman has pointed out, "Perceptions of past experiences are often filtered through a contemporary lens." The interviews, or monologues, presented in this book compose a chorus of voices whose lives have often been ground down by years of economic uncertainty. Long gone are the aspirations of their youth. They drive a cab not by choice but by necessity. The answers to the questions posed to them were often shaped by that resignation.

Parallel to this, a major hurdle with the research was finding willing interview subjects. As soon as a microphone was turned on the taxicab drivers were often unsure about the process, even after anonymity was guaranteed. In fact, it was explicit that details would be masked to hide their identity. This book does not name names nor does it target specific companies. Only several former and current stand owners and cab drivers are identified; the rest are pseudonyms. The book does, however, identify industry-wide problems.

The modern nature of the taxi business has made many drivers nervous. They fear retaliation from their employers as well as their co-workers. Even the Commission of Inquiry into the St. John's Taxi-cab Industry, established in 1990 to "complete a comprehensive review of the taxi industry and to determine the appropriateness of the existing Taxi Bylaw," couldn't get more than a few drivers to come forward to air their grievances. Instead, the city heard from the fleet owners and the brokers (a multiple-lease holder who rents his cars to taxicab drivers for an even share of the profits). This book lets the taxicab drivers of St. John's speak for themselves without fear of recrimination.

There are standby lots spread out all over the city, places where drivers wait for the dispatcher to send them on a job: strip malls, gravel patches just off the main roads, colleges and government buildings. Taxis wait at airports and at hotels with which the company has a contract. These were the sites of most interviews. Some were in homes; some were in coffee shops. As to finding interview subjects, a taxicab driver occasionally introduced a friend. Other drivers were approached blindly but often without much success.

Many interviews were conducted while the driver waited for a job. If one took place in a taxi, the driver sat alone up front and the microphone was placed on the armrest. When little or no background information was available, form questions were posed: *When did you start taxiing? What companies have you worked for? Has it been an enjoyable or negative experience?* While some interviews lasted for more than an hour—and a few taxicab drivers availed themselves for follow-ups—most spoke for just twenty minutes or so. The structure of the book was determined by those brief but highly informative interviews.

Only a few of the chapters within this book are life stories, or self-contained narratives. Most are snapshots of a specific incident gleaned from a longer interview. These monologues are divided by title but connected thematically, and they are often introduced by brief commentary. Oftentimes a taxi driver will speak more than once and at different points about a variety of subjects.

This book also addresses change in the periphery—the social, cultural and physical landscape of St. John's—and how the taxicab industry has adapted. Sometimes this change was technological, like the introduction of radios, fare meters and snow tires, while other times it was less tangible and more incremental, like the disappearance of the neighbourhood stands and the emergence of the fleets. But for the taxicab drivers themselves, working conditions have remained relatively static. Most are working poor, and few enjoy real job security. In fact, in some respects, conditions have worsened. Large fleets have consumed the vast majority of small taxi stands, creating a soft monopoly which contributes to the drivers' inability to affect change. In fact, outside of a handful of individually operated taxis, the neighbourhood stand has vanished. Taxicab drivers are no longer represented by a unified organization. The office of the taxi inspector, once a full-time position, has now been reduced to two Bylaw Enforcement Officers who are responsible for the administration of a whole host of municipal bylaws. Increases in drop rates, the amount one pays for just getting in a cab, play catch-up to inflation and operating costs.

This sample of interviews does not account for the working lives of all St. John's taxicab drivers. For some, it is a positive experience, reinforced by relationships formed with customers over years of reliable service, camaraderie with fellow drivers and economic independence. But these interviews do reveal that a significant number of taxicab drivers don't have the means to rise above the mire of the working poor, the dead end that can be driving a taxicab. The difficulty to earn minimum wage, despite working fifteen hours a day, seven days a week, was a recurring theme. One driver, a middle-aged former tradesperson who couldn't find employment in his field even with twenty years of job experience, said, "My wife once asked me why I keep at it. I told her, 'Because no one else will have me.'"

The Good Ol' Days

****

The Early Taxi Cab Industry

"In the old days, a fellow got big tips and didn't have to push a hack for sixteen hours; when he didn't have to fracture his skull climbing over a cab in front of him; when the streets weren't crowded with trucks and cars."

– Emil Hendrickson, New York cab driver,
from Graham Russell Gao Hodges,
Taxi!: A Social History of the New York City Cabdriver

The people of St. John's wouldn't have heard the word "cab" or "cabriolet" until at least 1820. It referred to horse-drawn carriages with two or four wheels, which seated up to four people. During the Victorian Era, the word "taxi" didn't mean much, either. Popularized in the United States, its origins are actually German. The "taxi meter," invented by Wilhelm Bruhn in 1905, recorded fares based on time and distance traveled. The word "taxicab" only became popular with the significant increase in automobile use in the early twentieth century. While the history books are pretty mute on the St. John's taxicab industry, we do know that by the 1860s cab stands appeared at Haymarket Square and Post Office Square on the east end of Water Street. By the 1870s, cabs had become so numerous that the city began the process of regulation. But that's where the historical narrative seems to end. Even the provincial and city archives are relatively silent on early taxicabs.

The story picks up again not long after automobiles began to appear in St. John's around 1905. Just prior to the First World War, the number of taxicabs operating in the city had grown enough that, in February 1912, the municipal council adopted "Cab Fare and Regulations for the City of St. John's." It required cab drivers to be licensed before plying for hire, to be eighteen years old and to have their cabs regularly inspected by a city official.

But that commercial activity held little resemblance to today's large fleets and brokerage system. Cabs were operated by one or two men who drove an automobile in the summer and, at the first sign of cold weather, put it into storage. A horse and side-sled were then used during the winter. At that time, Water Street and Duckworth Street were mud-clogged in the fall and spring and nearly impassable in the winter. The steep hills were treacherous, and the side streets were little more than pathways beaten down into the dirt. Automobiles simply couldn't get around. In fact, carriages operated well into the late 1920s. Anyone owning a cab went to the harbour and to the railway station on the east end of Water Street looking for a "hobble," or casual work. Some operated as tour cars. P. W. Patterson, who had a taxicab stand on the corner of Military Road and Gower Street, advertised his services in *The Evening Telegram*: "First Class Touring Cars, of high power, driven by expert chauffeurs for hire."

The first modern taxi stand to appear in St. John's was Station Taxi. Other stands soon followed—Grey Taxi, Blue Taxi and Hotel Taxi—expanding into what could be best described as a public utility. It was illegal for taxicab drivers to cruise for fares. To insure best mileage and easy access to customers, they stuck around the Post Office and the Courthouse, resulting in street congestion. For the first time, the city emerged from a passive role to impose some order on the industry by getting taxis off the main streets and limiting companies to five cars. A letter to St. John's City Council from the Department of the Colonial Secretary addressed their concerns: "For traffic purposes the cabmen now having stands in front of the Post Office and in front of the Courthouse should be removed from Water Street to some of the rear streets."

By the early 1930s, the country had plunged into the depths of the global economic Depression. Ninety thousand Newfoundlanders were on the "dole," or public assistance, with one third of the population living on 6 cents a day. In St. John's, unemployment was particularly visible. Throngs of men hung around the wharves and piers along the harbour, outside warehouses and on street corners. With no alternative for work, some turned to taxiing. At the height of the Depression, there were upwards of twenty taxi stands competing for hire where just five years before there were six. Many operated from residential homes while others had no known fixed address. Financially unable or unwilling to repair or replace their vehicles, unlicensed operators were continually entering and exiting the industry. They had become so numerous the city requested that the Newfoundland Constabulary "assist in rounding them up."

But then the Second World War all but eliminated unemployment in St. John's. The population grew by 11 per cent thanks to the "friendly invasion" of American, British and Canadian forces. According to historian Malcolm MacLeod, "The maximum number of American troops at any time came to 16,000; the Canadian total was slightly larger." By war's end, three quarters of 1 million troops had passed through American bases and installations.

For the taxicab industry, contracts with the American military meant big business. Stands began to pop up seemingly overnight. Some were operated from dispatch offices in backyard sheds; others, like Crown Taxi on Springdale Street, operated from makeshift booths alongside telephone poles. Larger companies like Burgess Brothers' Cabs took the opportunity to expand their business by more than doubling their number of licensed taxicabs and by building a garage to service them, common practice amongst taxi fleets in larger North American cities.

By the end of the war, the taxicab industry had ballooned to thirty-seven stands. By that time, the city was playing catch-up when it passed the "Taxi Bylaw" in November 1950, adapting existing regulations to meet technological advancements such as fare meters, better built cars and a swiftly urbanizing society. The bylaw made annual taxi driver licences and approved meters mandatory and set minimum employment standards for drivers (such as age and sobriety). Background checks prepared for the city by the Newfoundland Constabulary's Criminal Investigation Department are invaluable in revealing the social and economic backgrounds of taxicab drivers. The few available files—a brief selection from what must have been hundreds—indicate the applicants' addresses and job histories. Most were from the working class areas of St. John's. Some were veterans while others were unemployed tradesmen. The vast majority were men who had taxied prior to the war, and who, with few or no employment opportunities, returned to the one job where they knew they could make a dollar: taxiing.

The Last of the Old Taxi Men

Roy Burgess, son of Harry Burgess, owner of Burgess Brothers' Cabs

Parked in his son's garage is Mr. Burgess' first car, a '38 Nash. A taxicab sign is still attached to the roof, the original fare meter still in the glove box. On fine days, he takes it out to car shows, or parks it in front of his condo. It's a source of great pride. "She's the only antique taxicab in this city," he said. "My intent was to completely rebuild her. But my father said she wouldn't be an antique taxi if I did that. She had to be as she was then—original." Mr. Burgess is probably the last of the old taxi men. He witnessed the Depression, WWII and Confederation. WWII was an exciting time to be young in St. John's. For that generation, there was only one war, "The War." Mr. Burgess was in his early twenties then. His father, Harry, and uncle, Jim, were the owners of one of St. John's largest taxi companies, Burgess Brothers' Cabs. Career taxi men were once the norm, he explained. A man could make a decent dollar for himself and raise a family. It was a respected profession.

I suppose I'm the only old taxi man still around. I'm certainly the only one left in my family. My brother and sister are dead. My uncle Jim, who was in partnership with my father, never had any children. Harry Bugden and his daughter, Olive, are dead and gone. Doug Voisey—his father was Hotel Taxi—died of a heart attack.

Of the old taxi stands, the last was Burgess Brothers' Cabs, and we closed down in 1982. They were all taken over by people like the Gullivers and the Holletts. O.K. Taxi—that's another one that used to be big—didn't come into being until after the war. All of them that are in business today, like Northwest Taxi, have started up since George Street. Northwest Taxi was the old West End Taxi on Water Street west. They changed the name when they started operating from the Village Mall. Another one is City Wide. Dave Gulliver was originally in business with his father, which was Gulliver's Taxi on Queen's Street. Then he started his own stand and called it Dave Gulliver's Cabs. But Dave is only a young man compared to me.

Did I tell you how my father got into the taxi business? He decided he wanted to start taxiing, but he had no money. He went down to the Bank of Montreal on Water Street, walked in and said, "I want a loan of $500."

The bank manager asked him, "What do you want $500 for?"

"I want to buy a car to go taxiing."

"You're going to go into business by yourself?"

"Oh, yes."

"What collateral have you got?"

Now a man with Grade 5, what we used to call "primer," didn't know what the word "collateral" meant. He said, "What do you mean? What's collateral?"

"What value of the $500 have you got?"

My father said, "If I had the value of $500, I wouldn't be in here asking you for $500." He was right, as far as he knew. He had no education, or anything.

The bank manager turned him down: "We can't lend it to you."

Dad told him right to his face, "Go to hell!"

He walked out of the Bank of Montreal and went right across the street to the Bank of Nova Scotia. He told them the same thing—that he needed a loan of $500 to go taxiing.

They said, "You're going to make this a successful business?"

"Yes, sir."

"Here's your $500."

Years and years later, Mr. Ches Pippy, a well-known local businessman, rang the stand. He said, "Harry, we need a chauffeur for my Cadillac."

My father asked, "What do you want that for?"

"The president of the Bank of Montreal is coming to spend a week here. We need a chauffeur to drive him around."

"No trouble."

I became the chauffeur.

When it was all said and done, Mr. Pippy gave me an invitation to a big banquet on the final night the president of the Bank of Montreal was going to be in St. John's. I thought to myself, *What do I want to go to an old banquet for? I know my father won't go to no Bank of Montreal banquet.* But I brought the invitation down to the stand.

My father said, "Bank of Montreal? Not likely. Wait now. Yes, I'm going to go to that!"

He went down, walked in, and met the president. "How do you do? I'm Mr. Harry Burgess. I'm a successful businessman here in St. John's. I deal with the Bank of Nova Scotia."

The president asked, "Mr. Burgess, why do you deal with the Bank of Nova Scotia?"

"Because the Bank of Montreal turned me down."

Now is that an old-time story? It has nothing to do with the taxi business, but it does because that's how my father got started back in 1917. He would've been eighteen years old then. Now that's how far back the taxi business goes in my family.

In those early days, my father used a car in the summer and a horse and a side-sled in the winter. He operated down on Water Street right by the railway station. The horses were kept in a barn off LeMarchant Road. He told me that; I don't remember it. It was before my time. After all, I'm only eighty-odd years old. He used to go to the railway station and the harbour to pick up passengers. At times, there could be hundreds of people down there. Some came across the Atlantic from England and Europe and all those places. Some came from Nova Scotia and New York and Boston. He met all the Newfoundland coastal boats, too, like the *SS Kyle*. The cars would be all lined up, and the drivers would say, "Taxi, taxi!" In those days, that was part of your business. Those people needed taxis when they came to town. Nobody had a car. Even if they did, they weren't getting around. Sure, we never got our first snow plough until after the First World War. It was an old British tank. All they did was put a blade on the front of it. But that was no good because when she'd go down in a drift she couldn't get back up out of it. Eventually, they scrapped her for metal during the Second World War.

Later on, when the Newfoundland Hotel went up in 1926, my father and his brother and four others formed Hotel Taxi. They were Bugden, Voisey, Clooney and Dooley. That was so long ago now I can't remember their first names. But they were all taxi men trying to make a dollar wherever they could. They called it Hotel Taxi because it was on the side of the Newfoundland Hotel.

My father was the type of man who wanted to be on his own. When he started up at the Newfoundland Hotel, he had 500 people telling him what to do. But then war broke out in Europe. All of a sudden, business was booming. Fort Pepperrell (American Air Force Base) was here, and Buckmaster's (Canadian Military Head-quarters for Newfoundland) was here. But all he had was his car and his brother's car—that's it. He wasn't going to have that; he wanted to make money. "I'm not staying here with just two cars," he said. "Goodbye, boys."

The rest of them carried on, but they broke up after. The hotel said they no longer wanted a taxi stand on the side of their business. Voisey took the Hotel Taxi name, and he started up again on Queen's Road. Clooney and Dooley both got out of the business. Harry Bugden had nowhere to go; he had nothing. When Voisey moved down on Queen's Road, he didn't take Bugden with them. Old Harry Bugden couldn't get along with Voisey and them. He was a nice man, but he had his own ways.

When Burgess Brothers' Cabs started up in 1941, we were the first company in Newfoundland to call our cars "cabs." Everyone else used to call them "taxis." My father said, "We're going to call them cabs, just like they do in England." The building is still there. It's a restaurant today, but the original building is still there on Duckworth Street. We had a small garage, too. It was foresight on my father's part. He wanted to maintain his vehicles himself. There weren't many stands around with a garage. Crotty's Taxi was one. They had an old warehouse on Theatre Hill. Queen Street is what they call it today.

The war changed everything. That's when it got rough in town. The taxi drivers were always half-afraid with the soldiers getting drunk. In those days, no one ever hailed taxis. But if they called, you might get stuck with a drunken Canadian, or a drunken Englishman, and he might vomit up over the seats. Then the car would be out of commission all the next day getting cleaned. The Canadians coming off the ships were pretty terrible. The Canadian Army base was at Lester's Field. They were always drunk up there. The Canadian Navy was in Buckmaster's. The bases were supposed to be self-contained, but the soldiers were downtown all the time into the beer parlours. If someone rang us from Buckmaster's: "Oh, we haven't got a car." We didn't want to go up to Buckmaster's, or Lester's Field. In those days, you could choose your work because there was so much business. Why take the scruff? Take the good stuff.

If you got into trouble with Canadian servicemen, a drunken serviceman getting out of hand, you didn't ring the police, you rang the shore patrol—the Canadian Navy Shore Patrol. They patrolled around the city just as the police did. They'd just arrest them right away and make sure you got your money. They were good like that. They were next door to us, right where there's a tavern today. That was their jail. All night long they were hauling in the drunks off the ships, piling them in there to sober them up.

But you never had trouble with an American. The Americans wouldn't put up with their servicemen like that. They didn't take any shit from them at all. They wouldn't be out at night to the beer parlours because they had all their own clubs on the base. We got a lot of good work from the Americans. Fort Pepperrell was a big part of our business. We liked Fort Pepperrell because it was completely controlled. They were good people to deal with. A lot of Newfoundland men and women worked there, too, and they needed taxis to go to work and to come back home. We drove all of those people. The base might ring us and say, "We need three officers brought over to Argentia." Or they could ask us to pick up such and such and bring him back to the NCO club. Stuff like that. You had servicemen who were courting Newfoundland girls, too. An American soldier might want to go see some young woman. He'd ring us to go pick her up to take them to a movie, or a dance.

There weren't too many companies working on the American base. There was us and Hotel Taxi. The Americans were very choosy. You had to get a licence and get checked out and everything before you were even allowed on the base. There was a little bit of bootlegging—that sort of thing. But we never got involved in any of it. If the Americans found out you were bootlegging a bottle of rum and it was in your cab you'd never be allowed back.

The Americans were a different class of people than the rough-and-ready Canadian Army and Navy men. Even the Englishmen. All they were interested in was partying and drinking. The Americans weren't like that.

For us, the biggest challenge during the war was cars. You just couldn't get cars because there were no cars being made. You couldn't get tires, either. You could still get tires but you could only get so many a year—they were rationed. Tires didn't last like they do now, either. In those days, because of the gravel roads, they only lasted two or three months. Now you can get tires on your car that'll last two or three years.

You had to have synthetic tires on your car because that's all that was being made. Synthetic tires were tires that weren't made of rubber. They were synthetic. You could tell they were synthetic by the big round red dot on them. It was about the size of a half-dollar. If you had them on your car you weren't allowed to go anywhere the trains went. The trains were supposed to take the passengers. It was to save on tires—that was the rationale behind it. We'd have to keep the old pre-war worn-out regular tires to go back and forth to Argentia. But those jobs were good money. Thousands of men were out in Argentia. On the weekends, they weren't staying in Argentia, which was actually Placentia. There was nothing in Placentia. The big city was St. John's. What would happen was, the crowd would come into town on a Friday or Saturday, and they'd have to be back on the base early Monday. But the train didn't leave until seven o'clock in the morning. Half of those guys would be in St. John's, and they'd hire a taxi to go back out. A driver could go to Argentia and make himself $35.

In our day, the taxi business was a regular business with regular working hours. It was busy in the daytime. Half of our fleet would go on at eight o'clock in the morning. They'd go home to dinner at twelve and come back at one. When six o'clock came, they went home. On the weekdays, we stayed open until twelve at night. On the weekend, it was one. Beer parlours closed ten o'clock at night. Stores were only open Saturday night until nine-thirty. They closed on Wednesday afternoons. That's the way business was in those days. Grocery stores are now open seven nights a week. That's where the difference is between then and now.

The people in the taxicab business were elite people. Everyone went to work in the morning with a collar and tie and suit of clothes on. You were more like a chauffeur, not a taxi driver.

I remember a young man came into the stand and said, "Mr. Burgess, I want a job."

My father said, "Yes, my son, you go pass your driving test, you get a haircut and you arrive here with your collar and suit and tie on, and we'll give you a job."

"You can't make me get a haircut! You can't make me put a collar and tie on!"

"No, I can't," my father said. "But I can if you work for me."

When we hired a driver, he knew he was going to get a day's pay. An ordinary day back in the '40s and '50s was $35. There were twenty-five calls on a sheet. Most jobs were $1. It was $2 an hour waiting. After twenty-five runs, he was sure to make at least $25. But then a lot of jobs were $1.50, $2 and $3. When he added it up at the end of the day, a driver probably had $35. When a driver came in at nine o'clock, the first thing he did was fill the car up at the pump. That was written on his daily sheet which he passed along to the dispatcher. On Friday, all the amounts were made up, and 40 per cent was taken off for him. That's how he was paid. Sixty per cent went to us to maintain and repair the cars and to operate the stand. What brokers do now, they go fifty-fifty. It wasn't in our day. Forty per cent of what he took in was his, the driver's. Your unemployment and your taxes came out of it, and everything. It's all cash money now.

Maintenance wasn't a big cost to us. You could insure a car for $100 a year. Now it seems like you can't have a taxi on the road for $100 dollars a day. Maintenance only got bad in later years when the drivers didn't know how to drive and were breaking up the cars. If there was anything wrong with their car, the driver would tell us, and we'd fix it. When we decided a driver needed a new car we'd take that car and give them a new one. In fact, we changed our cars every two or three years.

But the type of driving then was completely different than it is today. You got guys speeding around on two wheels today. In our day, the speed limit was twenty miles-an-hour. You didn't break up a car at twenty miles-an-hour. If you hit a pothole, the car went down and then came back up out of it. There was no such thing as complaining about a pothole down the road because what was on the streets wasn't really pavement like we know it today. It was coal tar. Sand was put down, and then tar was put down over it. There were no paving machines. The first paved street we got in St. John's was King's Bridge Road, and the Americans did that. They brought in the machines from the States and made a concrete road right from the Newfoundland Hotel, what we used to call "The Hotel," down to the corner of the Boulevard.

The process of moving into today's taxi business—snow tires, electric meters, two-way radios and the expansion of the airport—I grew up with all of that.

I can remember when snow tires came out just at the end of the war. Terra Nova Taxi on Prince of Wales Street was the first company to have them.

Somebody said to my father, "Are you going to put snow tires on the cars?"

He said, "I'm going to put them on every one tomorrow."

"But they say they're not as good as chains."

"They're not as good as chains; they'll never be as good as chains. But what's the good of me being down at the bottom of Signal Hill with chains on and six guys in front of me stuck in the snow? How am I going to get up out of it? It's just as well for me to have the snow tires on, too."

Snow tires weren't a big expense. They were no more expensive than an ordinary tire. You always had a load of replacements in your garage, anyway. But then the drivers didn't have to get their clothes dirty jacking up the cars and putting chains on. With chains, every time a bar broke it hit the fender. That's a dent in your fender then. The chains only lasted a day, anyhow. A real busy day, that's all you'd get out of them. But with chains you could go up and down any hill in St. John's. You never had to worry. There was no sanding or anything like that. Snow ploughs only went around once a week.

Snow tires are what forced the roads to be better because you couldn't get around as good as when you had chains on. That's when the city started sanding the streets. Salting came in after. I think we were the only ones to have sanders in our cars. When it got too slippery going up over a hill, you pressed a button and she'd squirt out the sand in front of you from two little buckets that were in the trunk. It was the same as the big spreaders today. But they got worn out and clogged up. When the roads got better, we just discontinued using them.

In 1948, the first meter was brought in. It was a Cabbel Meter. I still have one in my '38 Nash. When we went into Confederation, the city decided to use a new Canadian-built meter called the Sivec. If you were a taxi driver, that's the one you used. Gordon Butler had the contract for them. He had an old stationery store on Water Street, Pens and Pence. But when he started installing the meters, he opened up a place on Hamilton Avenue. Because they were controlled by a clock, Dick Harris, a jeweller, became the man to do all the repair work on them. He made a dollar at it, too, because he was the only one who knew how to fix them, unless you sent them back to the factory.

Taxis had two-way radios before the police did. The first taxi company to have them in their cars was Mulroney's Cabs on Fleming Street. It helped a lot if you had to pick up a customer on John Street, for instance, but you couldn't find the address. You could always ring back to the stand for directions. It was convenience, more than anything else. Remember, you still had to go back to the stand after every run before you could get another job, but we often picked up those jobs on the sly, anyhow.

When you're an owner, you never had time to drive a cab eight hours a day. You had other things to do. I had a bit of an education and my father didn't. From 1948 right up until we closed in 1982— that's about thirty-five years—I did the bookwork and made up the paychecks.

I had my own business to run, too. I bought Silverlocks, an automotive store, when I was twenty years old. Then I bought out the Radiator Shop. I had an agency for taxi signs. I brought in the orange signs for Burgess Brothers' Cabs. Everyone else had white or yellow signs. The family, which included my uncle, too, had Tilden Rent-A-Car. We were all in it together, we'll say: Dad and his brother, and me and my brother and my sister.

That era was probably the peak of the taxi business in St. John's. I suppose I could name every taxi stand that was on the go then. Georgetown had Rawlins Cross Taxi and Mulroney's Taxi. Rabbittown was—I wouldn't say a slum—but a lower-class part of St. John's. It ran from Bonaventure Avenue where the St. John's Curling Club is today and then west on Empire Avenue. Empire Avenue was the old track; that's where the train came through. All up through Calver Avenue and Summer Street was Rabbittown. They were more or less poorer-type people with small houses. They had Terra Nova Taxi. Super and Ace were there, too. Then they combined and became Super Ace, which is today Co-Op Taxi. There was Blue Taxi by the post office. There was Hub Taxi, Square Taxi and Station Taxi. That was all between the west end of Water Street and the railway station. Then you had ones just off of Water Street on Adelaide: O.K. Taxi, Radio Cabs and Wheeler's Cabs. None of the stands had ten cars. Most of them had four. That was the standard size taxi stand.

One of the most famous taxi stands, I suppose, in those days, was O.K. Taxi. That was down on Waldegrave Street. In 1946, after Frank O'Keefe came back from the Second World War, he opened up O.K. Taxi. George Martin started that up. His father, Jake Martin, worked with us in Burgess Brothers' Cabs. He was a fine driver, too—a real Dapper Dan. He had to have his suit of clothes just so, and his tie was just so. George sold it all after, and he opened up Valley Cabs in Mount Pearl.

When Harry Bugden left Hotel Taxi he had nothing. He had no taxi stand. He got together with Jack Crosbie, who was in with the airport crowd. Bugden said, "Well, I got the experience in the taxi business. My name is popular. If I had the cars, I could operate a stand."

Crosbie said, "Okay, we'll get ten cars. We'll get ten Chevys— all light blue."

Then the tender came up for the airport, and he got it.

My father wasn't interested in it. He said, "Why do I have to be dictated to by an airport with ten cars and uniformed men when I got a nice little taxi business of my own? I'm not interested."

Frank O'Keefe: "Nah, I'm not interested."

Hotel Taxi: "Nah, I'm not interested."

Harry Bugden was down to the stand one day, and he was talking to Dad about different things. Dad said, "Harry, I don't know if this airport contract is as good as it's supposed to be. I could send in five cars to the airport for when a plane gets in. Each one of them picks up a passenger. But some of them got three and four passengers, and they're only paying a dollar each."

You see, City Council had made a law that said because it was the airport they could charge by the head and not by the meter, the same as the railway station. But today, the legal way in St. John's is if a passenger gets in a taxi you're supposed to turn on your meter. Say you take a customer up to Topsail, and they ask, "How much, please?"

The driver might say, "$40."

"Where's that on your meter, sir?"

"Oh, I didn't turn it on."

"Well, turn your meter on. How much is it now?" It'd be whatever the drop rate is. "$3.25? Well that's all I got to pay you. That's the law."

Driving around all the old drunks is what took the good out of the business. We didn't cater to that trade at all. We catered to the respectable trade: bringing people to church on Sundays, and all that good business.

That's the way the taxi business was run back then.

A taxi used to be a luxury. For instance, Mrs. Jones or Mrs. Murphy might ring us on Saturday night, and we would book them in to go to church Sunday morning. Or Mrs. Maloney or Mrs. Bowring might ring us up to go for a run around Marine Drive on Sunday afternoon. They would never want to see a sign on top of the car. They wanted to be sitting in the back, as if to say, "This is my car, and this man is driving me around." That's why it was called chauffeuring. O.K. Taxi had a fleet of Nash cars. One of their cars was white—the wedding car. That's all that car was used for. If you had a wedding tomorrow you had to hire a taxi because there were no cars around.

Ordinary people never used taxis. Everyone went on the streetcars or the buses. In fact, we had a good transportation system here in St. John's. It was called Golden Arrow Coaches. They had ten buses and a plough to clear the streets. The buses ran on Duckworth Street because there wasn't enough space for them to pass

the streetcars on Water Street. The streetcars were eventually retired because people started using the buses. Besides, the streetcars
were getting old, too, and Light and Power wanted to get rid of
them. The buses had four main runs: the west loop, the east loop,
the Grace Hospital and the General Hospital. The bus terminal was
on Harvey Road. During the war, when the Americans wanted
buses going to Pepperell, they got Golden Arrow Coaches to operate them.

Golden Arrow Coaches eventually went out of business and another mainland company came in, Capital Coach Lines. But they
couldn't make a go of it, either. The trouble was they didn't have
good buses. All they had was old school buses. It's the same as the
school buses today. All they got now are leftover buses brought in
from the mainland. The taxi business isn't much different. Bugden's
Cabs, when they were operating years ago, my God, they had a new
fleet of cars on regularly. We all brought in brand new cars. When
you were finished with them, anyone could have them. We didn't
care who had them. As far as we were concerned, they were worn
out. We made enough money on the year or two that we had them
to replace them. Now mostly what they got on the streets is old used
cars that they buy at auction.

The taxi business is still a good business, but it's not the pres-
tige business it once was. Today, it's a cutthroat boozers and drunks
business. I mean, take us, for instance. We had a direct line to the
Janeway. We took every call that came out of there. We did the Confederation Building up on Circular Road. In those days, it was called
the Canada House. We had a contract with CBC; we brought all
their reporters around. They never had their own cars, or anything.
That was all daytime work done by us.

We had the contract for the penitentiary. The guards put the
prisoners in the car, brought them to the railway station and then
sent them home. A lot of them were men from around the bay who
got put in jail for the winter because they liked three hot meals a
day. Half of them were in there for making moonshine and stuff
like that. That's half of the crooks that were in Newfoundland years

ago. The crooks weren't bad in those days. I suppose there were murders and all that every now and again, but there was nothing like the crimes you see on the news today. The city was much quieter.

One time, I met an old policeman who was a patient at the Miller Centre. I said, "I can't remember you on the police force." He told me his name. "Goddamn it! I do remember you. Do you remember Burgess Brothers' Cabs?"

"Yes, sir. Burgess Brothers' Cabs were the main taxi business in St. John's. That's the one we all honoured. If there was a crook missing we were trying to find, we rang Burgess Brothers' Cabs: 'Have an eye out for such and such.'"

When the nightclubs started up on George Street, all the good taxi stands went out of business.

In my day, there were only a few beer parlours in town. Cottage Gardens was on Merrymeeting Road. It was a beautiful building, an old-fashioned two-story building. No women were allowed in there because women weren't allowed in beer parlours. The nightclubs used to be outside the city limits. There was no nightclubs in St. John's. It wasn't allowed—that was the law. You had the Old Colony Club. You had the Bella Vista. You had the Commodore Club out by the airport. Then you had the Crystal Palace out in the Goulds. Out in Mount Pearl, you had the Old Mill.

The nearest nightclub was the Old Colony Club on Portugal Cove Road. It was the elite club. You had to be a member to go in there. The Goulds and all the rest of them were all regular nightclubs. Club 21 was another one on Topsail Road. It became Dominic's Place. If you took your girlfriend to the Old Colony Club, or the Commodore, or the Bella Vista, my God, you were taking her to the big dance. The nightclub was an elite business. People went into the Old Colony for their supper. There was a dining room just off the bar, or down the stairs was the dance hall. For some dances, you had to go in formal clothes—long dresses and tuxedos.

You never took your girlfriend into the beer parlour. That was never heard of. You took her dancing. You took her to a movie, or you took her parking. Cabot Tower is the famous place. Well, that was the famous place to go parking in those days. It was very romantic to bring your girlfriend up to Cabot Tower overlooking the city to see all the lights.

The Sundance would've been one of the first nightclubs on George Street. It used to be a garage, the old Adelaide Motors building. But George Street was nothing in those days, just a little place with a few taverns.

By that time, a lot of the drivers were terrible. They didn't know how to drive. They were driving too fast and skidding all the time. They were breaking up the cars.

I can remember my Uncle Jim saying down to the office, "I'm so Jesus fed up with this Jesus thing. I'd like to take every Jesus car down there off the road."

"What's wrong now, Uncle Jim?"

"Johnny such-and-such just broke up one of the cars again."

You know what I suggested? Sell the cars out to the drivers and let them do what they like. Just become a broker. And so he did. Uncle Jim arranged it all through the Bank of Nova Scotia. They lent the drivers the money, and Uncle Jim backed it. If they fell through on the loan he just took the car back and sold it to somebody else. But Uncle Jim didn't like brokering; he had no use for it. Uncle Jim was a businessman, like my father. He didn't want to see those cars come and go as they pleased. We were putting guys on for the night shift and only half of them would show up. Here's the dispatcher with a list this long, trying to please the customers but with no cars to do it.

Uncle Jim used to say, "I got fifteen cars that are supposed to be down here today, but I only got five. I can't tell the other ten they got to come in. They own their own cars. But I need to have cars on the stand if I'm going to make money."

The last fleet of cars we bought was in 1976—they were Chevy Malibus. We started selling them out as brokers in 1978, and we kept it going until 1982. But it got to the point where I was no longer interested in it. Besides, I had other businesses. Uncle Jim was up in his late '80s. It was just time for him to get out. Uncle Jim said, "To hell with it!"

It wasn't a taxi business any more, as far as we were concerned. The bottom had already dropped out of it.

It Was Steady Go—Steady Belt

Gerald, driving for forty-one years

Mr. Burgess witnessed what was, from his perspective, the devolution of the taxi business from a system of neighbourhood-based and family run stands into what would become a public utility dominated by soft monopolies. The career taxicab drivers quoted in the following monologues point out that for as long as they have been behind the wheel they've had to hustle to make a dollar both on and off the meter. Their livelihood has always depended just as much upon the daily routines of their working class customers as they have upon the city's vices.

There is little glamour in the taxi business, only pride. For those drivers who know nothing but being behind the wheel the stories of their early working lives are often humorous and full of youthful optimism. There is none of the cynicism of having been ground down by years of uncertainty and an income that has steadily diminished through increased stand rates, gasoline prices and insurance costs.

When I started driving in the early '60s, gas was 59 cents a gallon, and it was only $8 to fill up your tank. You could go from here to Gander and back—I've done it, gone out to central and back again in a taxi—and when I got back to the Crossroads the tank took $8.13. The meters had a big handle on them you had to wind. When you turned it up the meter was on. When you turned it down you were stopped. There was none of this waiting time, like when you're stopped at a red light. It was based on distance. The first half-mile was 70 cents, and every quarter mile after that you got 10 cents. You could go downtown for $1. You could go down over Barter's Hill to Woolworth's on Water Street and there would be $1.10 on the meter. People would get out on New Gower Street and walk over so they'd only have to pay the dollar.

If you went to Harbour Grace it was only $30, and that was a good run. Harbour Grace is now $146. It's $200 to go to Argentia, where it used to be $35. There used to be that much crushed stone on the Argentia Access Road that it took an hour and a half just to get down from the Trans-Canada Highway.

You'd make $100 a day. We were busy. It was steady go—steady belt. But that's when a dollar was worth a dollar. You went at it as fast as you could be at it because there was only one stand in the west end. There were no big stands like City Wide Taxi and Jiffy Cabs. City Wide only started up in the 1990s. Peter Gulliver's grandfather, Pearce Gulliver, had a place over on Queen Street. His son, Dave, went out on his own then and called it Dave Gulliver's Cabs because his father had the name Gulliver's Cabs. They had '69 Ramblers, twelve Rambler Rebels, and one Ambassador. Jiffy Taxi started in 1955. They only had five or six cars. I can remember that; I was ten years old. Then they closed up for years and years until Tom Hollett took it over.

You had a lot of taxi companies because not many had radios. Radio Taxi didn't even have a radio. You had to go back to the stand and wait for a job off the phone. If the phone rang ten after seven, they'd say, "That's missus so-and-so. She's going to bingo tonight."

You knew everybody you drove. You knew who it was before you picked them up. It was all regulars. We didn't have much of a tourism industry. The tourism industry only came here a few years ago. We had the people who came in on the flights and left and went out on the same night, or stayed overnight and went out the next day. We didn't have any tourists. Now you hardly see the same people.

I worked at other jobs, but they were seasonal. I worked the longshore for a couple of months every year when they were busy, and I worked for Molson driving the beer truck at Christmastime.

But I would always go back taxiing because that's where the money was. There was instant money. It was a good life because you always had money. There was no such thing as having to wait until Friday to get paid. If you started a job today, they'd hold back the first two weeks' pay. You got to go a month before you get a check. What would you do in a month? A month is a long time when you got no money. Even if they held back a week, that's still a long time to go with no money. But at this here you always got cash money. That's never changed.

I raised three boys. I never wanted for nothing. If I needed money, I'd go to work. Some people say taxi drivers are like fishermen, poor fishermen. But that's not true. That's definitely not true. Why would anyone be at it if they weren't making a dollar?

The Best Taxi Driver in St. John's

Theodore, driving for thirty-eight years

Jimmy Stone used to be a popular name in the taxi business. When he was at it, he was probably the best taxi driver in St. John's. I saw him one time driving this older lady up to Sobeys on Ropewalk Lane. He got her walker out and helped her in. He sat her on the bench and told her to wait there while he parked the car.

I was out by the door with the wife. I said, "Jimmy, what are you at?"

"I'm going in to help her buy her groceries."

When he came out, he put the bags in the trunk, took her home and put her groceries away for her in her cupboards. Jimmy used to do that, and with some guys you can't even get them to open a door for the customer. They wouldn't care if you were 100 years old, they wouldn't get out and help you with nothing. Jimmy was a taxi driver, buddy, I guarantee you. He was a gentleman.

The Taxi Inspector

Darryl, driving and dispatching for twenty-five years

It was five bucks for your taxi licence and twenty-five to register the car. The city would give you a big card that used to go in the window and a separate card for your pocket. You got one every year. You had to go down to the Horseshoe Tavern and get the taxi inspector. That was in the 1960s before City Hall was built. City Hall wasn't built until the 1970s. He would spend all day into the Horseshoe Tavern drinking beer. Beer was only 33 cents a bottle. You could buy three for $1 and get a penny back.

There was no paper record of you getting your licence because he spent the $5 on beer. But then computers started to come into it and there was a record kept of everything.

The Knight Riders

Edward, driving for thirty-eight years

What got me into this headache? My father was poisoned with me going to him for money. "This is what you're going to do," he said. "You're going to get a taxi licence."

The Mounties took me out for my driving test. I drove around Pleasantville and parked between two cars. But when I went to back her out, I forgot she was still in reverse and struck the pole. The Mountie said, "Don't worry, it was my fault. I distracted you."

Frank Upshaw was doing the hiring for Gulliver's. "See Bill Grouchy at City Hall. Tell him you want your taxi licence."

I showed Bill my driver's licence, and he wrote out a card and stuck a little silver dash on it. "Go to work," he said.

That was in 1974. I've been at it ever since.

For my first job, I drove some buddy out to Mount Pearl, and he stuck me for the fare. At least, he tried to stick me for the fare. He got out and walked up to his apartment. I can still see him as plain as day. He said, looking down, "What are you waiting for? You're not getting paid."

"Say that to my face," I said.

He ran down over the stairs and hauled out a wad of cash and started waving it in my face.

I was sitting in the front seat, grabbed him by the scruff of the neck and took the money and shoved it in my mouth. "You're not getting that," I said. "Thank you."

I ended up giving him a good knocking. But, man, he was as tough as nails—as tough as nails. When I got back into the car, he was getting up, and grabbed me by the jean jacket. He ripped the back right off, the square piece on the back of the jacket.

When I pulled out, he chased me with the piece of my jacket in his hand: "I'm going to kill you. *I'm going to fucking kill you!*"

I still got my money, though.

You look back on those kinds of things and kind of laugh.

When I started driving, I never had any kids, and I wasn't married. I had lots of time on my hands and cash in my front pocket. I was meeting all kinds of different people and getting paid for it. I was happy to get behind the wheel of a taxi and drive someone to work, pick them up and bring them home, or drive them to the supermarket, the hospital. It wasn't like working in an office where you got to stick inside all day. You could come and go when you pleased. You could go home when you wanted, go pick up a bucket of chicken, or grab a beer if you wanted. Drivers weren't under as much pressure and stress as they are now, either. At the end of the day, I can't wait to get out of the car. It gets to you because you know you got to be out and there's nothing else for you but taxiing.

There was a television at the stand where you could watch a bit of the news while you waited for a job. You could go in and watch television, relax, and have a cigarette and a coffee. All the drivers got along because there weren't a lot of cabs on the road, and everyone was getting their fair share of work. There was no Jiffy. There was no Co-Op. ABC was on the go over on Southside Road, but they had maybe only fifteen or twenty cars. Courtesy Taxi only had five cars, and so did Golden Cabs. It was easy to make money because everyone worked a particular area. Golden Cabs had

Churchill Square. Bugden's had the east end. There were only ten cars down to Gulliver's, whereas now they got close to ninety. You were working with a good bunch of guys who would take the shirt right off their back and give it to you. There was no job robbing, no fussing.

Johnny Dunn, the little midget, is dead now. But when he was dispatching, if a job was given to you on the stand to pick someone up, but there was already a car in the area, Johnny would say, "What do you want to do?" You would pass the job onto that driver. That was common. There was no robbing jobs on other drivers, and there was a very slim chance of getting a water haul—going to a house and no one comes out. There was none of this calling up two or three different companies on a Friday or Saturday night and taking the first one that got there.

We really had to work the hours, but that's never changed. I had to put in ten, twelve, fifteen hours a day, just to stay on top. I ate, slept and breathed in the car. There was none of this airport stuff, hooking jobs to Clarenville, Gander, or Bay Roberts—a big score. You were tickled pink to drive a parcel up over the hill for $3. Right now, the meter starts at $3.25, but gas is more expensive. It used to be $5 for a half-tank of gas, and insurance was dirt cheap. I think I was paying $500 a year when I first put my taxi on the stand—probably less.

Rather than wait for a job from the dispatcher, I'd cruise. He would write you down on a piece of paper and if you didn't get a job off Water Street he'd give you a house job. But Water Street was always flat out. Woolworth's was the busiest department store in the city. Then there was The Arcade and Bon Marche. Those stores were open for years, long before I was born.

George Street was nothing, a ghost town. There was a supermarket and a scrap metal shop, and that's about it.

Water Street was the thing for taxi drivers.

When I got put on nights, it was like a whole other world. I was used to picking up people at Woolworth's and The Arcade. When the supermarket was on Parade Street, I would pick up customers with a load of groceries. I had never experienced night driving. I said to myself, *This is wicked!*

Fact was, you're making more money and you're into the downtown scene.

I learned pretty quickly that part of driving the night shift was hustling to make a dollar off the meter. I often had prostitutes in the car. Sometimes I'd drive them over to Confederation Building, and they'd take buddy with them and go lie down in the field for fifty bucks. They weren't up there with those fancy girls, the call girls, or whatever it is you call them. They were at the bottom of the ladder—they were desperate. There was a whole load of them around Bulger's Lane. The Portuguese and Japanese fishermen would come off the boats and they would give you fifty bucks for lining them up with a prostitute. Every driver knew where they were to, them and the bootleggers. If those same fishermen wanted a bottle of rum after eleven o'clock, you would bring them up to Shea Heights. If they wanted a woman and a bottle of rum, you'd take them up to Shea Heights and then back to Bulger's Lane. Then he's got his bottle of rum and his woman.

For me, how I remember it, Water Street in the summertime was like Hollywood Boulevard. People would be lined up on the sidewalks waiting to get into the clubs. I'd have the windows down, the music going, waiting for a lady to stick out her leg, some beautiful blonde with a frame on her like a model. That's the one you watched out for. You're looking out the window, doing probably seven miles-an-hour because the traffic is bumper to bumper, and then out she steps with the red dress and the high heels and all done up to the nines.

That's when I had long hair and a full mouth of teeth. I would pick young women up down around The Stetson, some woman who has had a fight with her husband or her boyfriend. They would stand around and have a cigarette and look for meat and watch you cruise by. You'd probably go past her three times and she would still be on the sidewalk, watching. As soon as they got in the cab, first thing, they would ask how old I was. They would ask if I was married, or if I had a girlfriend. Then they would want to know if I was interested in coming in for a drink. Picking up a woman was something I had never experienced.

As a matter of fact, I picked up a crew at the airport, an Air Canada crew. There were three women. They were talking back and forth in French, and one of them said, "Listen cabbie, I'm sure you must know where to get some special stuff."

"What do you mean, special stuff?" I asked.

"You know what I mean. The good stuff."

"Yes, I know where to get it."

"I'll tell you what," she said. "You drop these ladies off at the hotel and we're going to go party. Don't worry about the fare. I got that covered."

"Go on," I said. "Fine and dandy."

The first place I hit was the Corner Tavern on Hayward Avenue. Dry. I went to Gower Street. Dry. I went to Froude Avenue. Dry.

"I don't know what to tell you, missus. This doesn't happen very often. I usually know where to get a few draws."

I got hold of Baker on the stand. We used to talk in this lingo where nobody could pick up on what we were saying. "Baker, where can I get a bit of ice cream, or cotton candy?"

"Go up to Empire Avenue and wait on the corner."

I went up and parked with her for five or ten minutes and three guys walked out from behind a house. I blew the horn to call them over, and she bought $100 worth of gear from them, which was a good bit of dope for that kind of money.

"We got to sample this," she said. "Let's go somewhere."

"Are you serious?"

"We got to sample this before I go back to the hotel."

We went up to Signal Hill, and I took a right by Deadman's Pond. We went in where there's a view of the harbour. "Down around the rocks" is what we used to call it. I put two cigarette papers together, rolled them up as thick as my thumb. "Do you really want to smoke this?"

"C'mon," she said.

We were having a puff and handing it back and forth, and then she wanted me to meet the other two: "Come in and meet my friends. One is from Nova Scotia and the other is from Montreal." That's why they were speaking French. I went in and sat down. They had wine in there, all kinds of drinks, and then she hauled out the bag of dope.

The music was going, they were laughing, carrying on, and they were starting to get pretty damn frisky, and I got right paranoid. "I got to go back to work," I said. "That's it for me—I'm gone."

If I told some of the younger drivers the stories I'm after telling over the years they wouldn't believe a word of it.

It used to be fun and enjoyable to drive a cab. Maybe that hasn't changed for the younger guys out on the road. Maybe I'm just out of the loop where I'm older. Michael O'Brien started down there with us, and he would tell you the same thing. He had his hair down over his back, too—real long hair—and gold on every finger and around his neck. Remember that show that used to be on television with the fast car that could talk, *Knight Rider*? That's what we used to call each other, "The Knight Riders." If you worked nights, that's what you were called. That atmosphere is gone. As far as I'm concerned, taxiing is only good for a nineteen or twenty-year-old.

Concrete Jungle

Michael, driving and dispatching for thirty-six years

I used to love for a Friday night to come. That was your money night. Saturday night was the same way. But you didn't have the cluster on George Street like you do now. We'd go and park at the Bella Vista. We'd go park at the Steamer. We'd go park at the Traveler's Inn. The clubs were spread out. You only had so many taxis this end of town, and only so many taxis that end of town.

It's like a concrete jungle down there now. Everybody is let out at one time and, you know yourself, you got thousands of people

27

on George Street between two and four in the morning. The more decks they put on, the more buildings they open up, the worse it gets. Ten years ago, Shamrock City was a jewellery store. Now it's a bar. All that along there on Water Street, the Post Office, what is it now? Dooley's. The list goes on and on. Years ago, they had the El Tico and a couple little small bars. Mostly there were department stores and restaurants. In around the corner, you had Gosse's. What could Gosse's hold? Probably twenty people. Sterling's was the same way. If you had ten people in there she was full. Some of the bars down there now can hold 1,000 people, I'm sure.

The only thing you had to contend with was a guy not paying you, or something like that. If you went to his house the next day, he gave you your $20. There are guys in this town that had hard names when I was taxiing. I know they don't mind me mentioning them: the Drukens, the O'Driscolls, the Mahers, the Leonards. If they didn't have any money or were that drunk they didn't know they were even in the cab you'd just bring them up to their door and they'd go on in. The next day, you'd get the money off them at their house, or you might see them on the street somewhere.

I never had a problem where I had to call the police. I was never assaulted. I never had any problems like that. If you went over to Gosse's or the Queen's Tavern, or any of the older clubs, and got a guy who you figured was too drunk you'd just leave him there with the bartender. But nine chances out of ten you were after driving him home within the last week, and you knew where he lived. Now his wife might not be very happy about it. I brought a guy up from Gosse's to Holloway Street. He had two bottles of rum with him. I opened the door, but she wouldn't let him in. She broke the two bottles of rum right there on the sidewalk. She wouldn't let him in, and he was no good to me. I ended up taking him back downtown and having the Constabulary look after him.

Anyone you interview in this city, anyone at all, will tell you it'd be worth it to sit on the roof of City Hall and look out and see what goes on Friday and Saturday night. If I'm coming up and I got you and your wife in the car and there's three or four guys who wants to get in with you, they're hauling open the doors, they're jumping up on the bonnet, they're holding onto the bumper.

That's why I'm dispatching. I'm too old for that kind of stuff. It's not fit down there—not fit.

Dead Time

Financial Hardships

"One thing about being a cabbie is that you don't have to worry about being fired from a good job."
– Alex Reiger (Judd Hirsh), *Taxi*

"Neither the company nor the union gives a damn about us. As far as they're concerned, we're machines—as wretched as the cabs."
– Lucky Miller, New York City cab driver, from Studs Terkel, *Working*

"We are all born poor."
– Rise Mickenber, *Taxi Driver Wisdom*

In the public's mind, the St. John's taxicab driver personifies both the real and the imagined ills of North America's oldest city. Whereas their habitat was once defined by the harbour and the railway station, it now encompasses the back lot of the airport, Water Street and Adelaide Street, and dozens of strip malls. These are often lonely and sometimes violent places. The popular image of the St. John's taxicab driver is blue-collar and itinerant, if not criminal and low-life. But their backgrounds are often working class and lower middle-class. Unlike most major mainland cities where upwards of 50 per cent of taxicab drivers are from predominantly Muslim countries, the St. John's taxicab industry remains largely ethnically homogenous: students, pensioners and the sons and daughters of taxicab drivers. Many are career drivers; few are women. Some, let go from other work, are too old and undertrained to re-enter the workforce, and they drive a taxicab as a last resort.

The taxicab industry, once a collection of family-run and neighbourhood stands, at its peak, in the years following the Second World War, counted forty-one taxicab stands operating within the city limits. Twenty-five years later, that number had dropped to thirty. Now there are just seven. What happened in the intervening years? As operating costs soared, older drivers and small fleets left the industry and sold their taxicab licences to larger stand owners. The 1970s also saw the emergence of the "broker," an independent contractor or middle-man, who had acquired small fleets and then leased cars to individual drivers for an even share of the profits. By the early 1990s, a handful of companies had grown to encompass three quarters of cab licences.

As in many other municipalities, leasing doomed many vulnerable drivers to a kind of wage slavery. At the end of the day, drivers are paid 50 per cent of whatever has accumulated on the meter, minus gas expenses. This was an obvious attraction to fleet owners and brokers because it ensured daily receipts and removed the spectre of rising gasoline and insurance costs. Individual taxicab owners, generally referred to as "independent operators," became subject to exorbitant and unregulated weekly stand fees. Although the 1990 Commission of Inquiry into the St. John's Taxi Industry found that stands were making only a modest return on their investments, the taxicab industry is largely cash-based. The Taxi Bylaw requires daily income sheets to be kept, but those rules are not strictly enforced.

To maintain a competitive environment while offering the public an adequate level of service, the city has periodically capped the number of available operator licences. Currently, there are 364. Although there is no uniform policy in place to determine the appropriateness of the number—municipal documents indicate one taxicab per 500 residents—it is reviewed by the Taxi Commission annually. Each stand owner must first purchase a stand licence that approves the operation of the stand and sets space requirements for its taxis. While the city has never restricted the number of taxicab stands, it has limited the number of parking spaces (referred to in the industry as "slots") to 402. While this regulation, in theory, offers owner operators some flexibility to move between stands, the reality is much different. The Commission of Inquiry determined that the regulations unfairly bind an independent operator to a stand, and that the opportunity to move was "exceptionally small and in most cases not practical." One taxicab driver spoke candidly about switching stands: "What's better, the devil you know, or the devil you don't know?"

Stand owners maintain that they play the necessary role of disciplinarian. In a brief prepared for St. John's City Council in June 1987, the United Taximen's Association, a now extinct stand owners' advocacy group, stated that this aspect of ownership "ensured good taxi service to the public." However, drivers are sometimes subject to the removal of equipment, arbitrary dismissal and blackballing, or collusion amongst stand owners. Beginning in the mid-1970s, the city permitted each stand to hire up to three part-time drivers. Now the taxicab industry depends upon a steady stream of these drivers, hired at the discretion of the stand owner, broker or independent operator, and whose income and record of employment often goes undocumented. This lack of regulation and entry level training encourages low standards of employment and a seemingly limitless pool of drivers operating around the clock.

Inadequate car maintenance is another serious problem. Pressured by high insurance premiums and other exorbitant start-up costs, few taxicab drivers buy new cars and many are stretched beyond 300,000 kilometres. In fact, high mileage automobiles are often purchased at auction, and regular maintenance is sometimes curtailed because of slim profit margins. Poor suspension and bad brakes are not uncommon. One driver explained, "The cars are complete junk. The owners don't care what happens to nothing. They got to get their cars moving."

The taxicab industry was once administered by a full-time inspector. But the bylaw sets only minimum standards for the conduct of drivers and the acceptance of vehicles as taxicabs. Currently, two enforcement officers are responsible for issuing licences, investigating complaints and ticketing bylaw infractions for the Department of Building and Property Management. With limited manpower and resources, it's often difficult to ensure that stand owners and brokers are meeting basic standards. This invariably affects the quality of service provided to the public.

St. John's taxicab drivers have made several attempts to mobilize their ranks. The United Taxi Drivers' Association, formed in 1985, had as its stated purpose to "promote the welfare of the members of the association with a view to enhancing their business" and to "examine problems pertaining to the operation of taxis." They had hoped to create a balance of power between stand owners, brokers and taxicab drivers. But taxicab drivers have always been difficult to organize. The highly competitive nature of the industry is a dividing force. Drivers are also physically separated from one another, creating an isolating work environment. Co-Op Taxi Ltd. emerged as a response to the failure of the association to force real change upon what taxicab drivers saw as an "industry in crisis." Owned and operated by taxicab drivers, their goal was to help reshape their public image and, through a cost-sharing model, increase their constantly diminishing profits.

Failing to find consensus and solutions, beginning in 1989, the city conducted a Commission of Inquiry into the taxicab industry. The Commission spent a year consulting drivers, brokers and stand owners, as well as the public, and reviewing the appropriateness of the bylaw. The final report, released in late 1990, dealt with issues that had dogged the industry for decades. Improving the quality of drivers, reversing the system of servitude to stand owners, and clarifying licence ownership were given top priority. Council considered a number of changes: returning the taxicab inspector to a full-time position, beefing up its role as a regulator and starting to test taxicab drivers' skills and knowledge of the city and safety. After two months, *The Evening Telegram* reported that only one recommendation had been implemented. The city continued to drag its feet, and little was ever accomplished.

For decades, St. John's taxicab drivers have been pushed to the fringes of the working poor and alienated from other working class professions. They are financially marginalized by what the Commission of Inquiry defined as "economic servitude," employment uncertainty and poor working conditions. Their wages remain static while gasoline and insurance prices continue to rise with inflation. Although there have been attempts at reform, little has changed since the late 1970s when brokers became the dominating force in the industry. During his mid-twenties, one informant drove a taxicab while he attended trade school. He said, "I got tired of sitting in the car for hours on end making next to nothing." It's a common theme. Amongst the drivers interviewed, long hours are a necessary part of a job that more often than not pays less than minimum wage. The problem is "dead time," the tiresome minutes and hours between jobs. If a driver starts his shift at six in the morning, it's not uncommon to have had only three or four customers by noon, which amounts to less than $100.

Sacrifices

Jacob, driving for two years

In the overflow parking lot at the St. John's International Airport, upwards of thirty cab drivers wait their turn to head down and park in front of the entrance. Only three cars are allowed there at any given time. They all hope for the "big score," a run that will take them out of the city and onto the highway. A sheet is provided to them by their employer and held to the sun visor with elastic, or stuffed in the glove compartment, which lists prices corresponding to communities. One driver brought a passenger to Corner Brook through a snowstorm for more than $1,000. But those kinds of jobs are a rarity—one in a million.

Driving a taxicab is not all that glamorous. Jesus Christ, in eight hours, I've made $63. At the end of my shift, after I gas up, I get half of what's left over. Do the math on that. I'll get about twenty-seven bucks for twelve hours work. For me, it passes the time. I'm a people person; I like people. When I went to university, my psychology course, which I passed, opened my mind to a whole new way of thinking. I like driving. It gives you something to do. It beats going to jail. It beats breaking the law.

The only people who are making any kind of money driving taxicabs are the guys who own their own cars. Guys like me who work for the company, the only person we're making rich is the man who owns the company. That's why they can have ninety cars on the road. If you're content to come out and pass away some time and bring home forty or fifty bucks on a good day, then that's okay. But it can be very depressing, this business, especially with all the cars out on the back lot here now. There's nothing on the set. There's no one phoning in. You might as well sit here and wait for a job that's going to Gander. I've been out eight hours, and I've got $23 on the meter, plus two twenties. Like I said, sixty-three bucks. I'll get down to the front of the airport, and the customer will probably say, "I'm heading to the Comfort Inn." You sat for three hours, and he wants to go to the Comfort Inn, which is right there, for ten bucks. And then they bitch about the price. If the radio is going, there's no sense even being at the airport. You've been sitting in my cab for ten minutes. The radio is working, and you haven't heard anything come out of it, have you? Not very much. So you sit, and you wait.

I make enough money to pay my rent and to pay my bills. I drive a school bus, and that helps. I'm separated from my daughter's mother, and I pay child support. I'm also paying for a couch so my daughter has some place to sit. The old couch was garbage. I had to buy something else and I'm not even living with them now. But I still went over to Easyhome. I'm paying forty bucks a week so my little girl can have some place to sit. I eat once a day. That's the truth. Yesterday, I had a slice of pizza at about two-thirty in the afternoon. I haven't eaten since. Sometimes you have to sacrifice.

Raising a Family

Mark, driving for twenty-one years

I got two little girls. One is thirteen, and the other is eight. My oldest daughter is in Grade 7, and my youngest is in Grade 3. To get them ready for back to school I had to punch in a lot of hours. You don't know from one day to the next what you're going to make. You could make $400; you could make twenty bucks. There's no set pay at this. That's about the worst thing about the job. You're gone from home a fair bit, too. But I try to be home as much as I can. I'll go home for a couple of hours here and there in the evening to spend a bit of time with the family.

Typically, I do six days a week. I usually come to work at about eleven o'clock in the morning and work until probably two or three that night. You're looking at fifteen hours a day six days a week. That's eighty to ninety hours per week. By the end of the week, I've almost always made the same amount as the week before. It usually works out that way—there's not a lot of variation. Some days you might have less; other days you might have more. I got two kids and a mortgage. Taxiing is not a gig where you can go home at five. You got to stay out until you make your money.

My family understands. They'd like it if I was home more, but they know that's not how it's going to be. I simply can't afford to be home more. These days it's a challenge for anyone with kids.

My father has been driving a cab for forty-five years. When I was growing up, he was gone a lot, too. He used to come home when he could, but he wasn't there every evening. I just remember he was gone almost all the time working. I don't know if it wasn't as busy then and it was harder to make a dollar. I haven't asked him. It's not a conversation that we've ever had. I was thirteen when my parents split up. So he lost a relationship over taxiing. I've thought about changing jobs. I was an electrician for a while before I started at taxiing. I did an electrical course at trade school back in the early '90s, but there was no work. That's when I started driving at Valley Cabs. For a span of about four years, I worked as a dispatcher for a courier company. That was a nine-to-five job. But I struggled with the routine. After doing this, I found I didn't want to be bound to an office.

I manage to leave my job in the driveway when I go into the house. I've been married fifteen years, and I don't think I spent ten minutes talking to my wife about this. It's just something I don't talk about. It's not something that interests her, and there's stuff that goes on that you got to deal with that I don't want her knowing about. With the girls, they don't usually ask too many questions. They know the hours I punch, and they know that this is Daddy's job. But that's the extent of it. It's not something that I ever get into. I'm not sure it's something I actually want to discuss with my daughters.

I mean, all you got to do is turn on the news to see St. John's is starting to get some bigger problems with crime and things like guys getting held up and assaulted.

A couple of years ago, I picked up three young guys, and they wanted to get dropped off at a gas station. They went in and came out with a bag of cigarettes, a couple cartons of cigarettes. I had to take them to another location, and they went in and came out with money, or whatever. They used a stolen credit card to buy the cigarettes. I didn't realize this until about halfway through that something wasn't adding up, something wasn't right.

I just didn't feel safe with these guys. It's just one of the times you get a bad feeling. I'm at this a while, and it's not often that I get spooked. One of the guys in the back never said a whole lot, but he was watching me. I thought, *If any trouble happens, this is the guy who is going to cause it.*

I've never mention anything like that to my wife.

Self-Discipline

Johnny, driving for three years

When you drive a taxi you can leave whenever you want. You can take your breaks whenever you want. You got to have a lot of self-discipline; you got to put the hours in. If you happen to leave you might miss out on one of the corporate jobs. We drive for Cougar Helicopters. You might hook a run with one of those guys going out to Bay Roberts. That's a $300 fare. But you got to wait that extra hour sitting down doing nothing. In the winter, there are your slow months. March and April gets pretty scanty. You're hunched over in the front seat, you got gloves and a hat on, and you're blowing on your hands trying to stay warm. You run the car for ten minutes, and you turn it off for half an hour. You turn it on for ten minutes, and turn it off for half an hour. So you're steady starting and stopping.

I quit doing day shifts because I was out one Monday and made $25 for an eight hour shift. I had to halve that with buddy who owned the car and then put gas in. You want to say, "I'm quitting this right now." But you got to take the good times with the bad. During the last George Street Festival, I made $2,800 in seven days.

The State of the Economy

Allen, driving for twenty-two years

Whatever happened to the blue collar jobs, the middle-class jobs? You either make ten to twelve bucks an hour, or you make $30 an hour. There's no twenty to twenty-five dollar an hour jobs out there. There is no blue collar, middle-class jobs out there, anymore. The state of our economy is fucked. I was making $50,000 a year. My employer made my job redundant because he could hire someone fresh out of school for $25,000 a year because they have less salary expectations, as opposed to me who is twenty years older. The whole concept of society here in Newfoundland is that you're either poor or you're rich. There's no in between.

All They Were Interested in Was Eating

Charlie, driving for thirty-seven years

Back in the '80s, all the old guys who were sixty and seventy grew up during the Depression. In the 1930s, if you're twenty-something years old, what's your biggest priority in a depression?

Putting food on the table.

You're fucking right, buddy. You got to eat. If you got a family, they got to eat. What do you do? You worked. Do you get an education? No, sir. That's the last thing on your mind. You're in Grade 2? Get out and go to work! And there are guys who will tell you that. For the guys who grew up in the Depression, all they were interested in was eating.

So back in the '80s, these old guys were driving around town. They knew the streets, not by their name, but by location. You see what I'm getting at? They knew where New Cove Road was. They knew where it started, and they knew where it ended. But they couldn't read the sign.

It might've been May 24th. It was a holiday weekend. I remember it was a cold night, but there was no snow, or anything. The dispatcher sends this old guy up to Cherry Hill Road. It was just up from New Cove Road there. I think it was maybe number sixteen, or something.

The dispatcher gives out a few more jobs over the set. About a half an hour goes by. He said, "I got that lady on the phone. Are you up on Cherry Hill Road?"

"Oh, yes," the driver said.

"Well, I got her on the phone, and she can't see you."

This driver got little or no education—he can't read. "Well, I'm here."

"Are you out in front of sixteen?"

"Oh, yes," he said. "I'm out in front of sixteen."

"That lady can't see you. You got to be on the wrong street."

"No," he said, "I'm not."

"Go to the end of the street, and spell the street name."

A minute later: "Go ahead, Bobby. I'm here."

"Spell out what's on the sign."

"S-T-O-P."

Cut Off at the Knees

Leonard, driving for four years

Few of the taxi drivers admitted to being behind the wheel by choice. For them, there is a lingering resentment for the life they once had or the possible future that slipped from their grasp: the agricultural plant manager, a victim of downsizing; the assembly line worker too broke up and worn down to keep working. One said, "There are firemen and teachers at it. There are a lot of retired people driving taxis. There are unemployed tradesmen at it. When a taxi hauls up to your door, you don't know who is going to be your driver. It could be the most educated man you've ever met, or the lowest form of human life."

Are you familiar with the Cameron Inquiry? I was the witness who had the mysterious piece of equipment. They wanted to know how I got it and what had happened to it. Apparently, there was a computer in the machine with patients' records. But like I told them, I didn't even know about the computer until I saw it on the news. For years, I worked on my own, selling and repairing new, used and refurbished medical equipment. Basically, anything and everything with a plug. I was generally referred to as a "field service technician," "field service representative," or "field service engineer." Take your pick—they all mean the same thing. I wasn't making a big lot at it, but I was making a damn size more than I am taxiing.

Everything that Eastern Health got rid of, I was the last stop before the dump. What you got to understand is when a machine became redundant and had to be replaced, they would keep the old one around for several months to make sure that the new one was working. When they determined their new machine was working properly, the old one got tossed. If I didn't take it, it was going to the dump. Say your wife wants to renovate your kitchen. After you get it half done, she says, "We need to get a new fridge and stove." What do you do with your old fridge and stove? You check to see if any relatives want it for their cabin, or something like that. Two weeks later, the fridge and stove is still sitting in the kitchen. Then the wife decides she's going to throw the things out. That's exactly what they used to do in the hospitals.

A lot of the instruments down there were worn out. Seven to ten years is the average lifespan of a piece of equipment. God only knows how long some of that stuff was down there. Take a family of twelve, for instance. How long is that washer and dryer going to last in their house? Not very long. If you have a family of four, you'll probably get ten years out of it. A family of twelve won't. That's what it was like for a lot of the stuff at Eastern Health.

I know we're not talking about the taxi industry here. I'm just trying to explain to you how I got back into it. The short order of it is I had no other choice.

I had taken this autostainer about five years before the inquiry started up. They asked me if I wanted it: "Get it out of our way."

I made a living the best way I could. I knew the instrument had some value, and I didn't want to see it go to the landfill. If that machine had been absolute garbage, I would still have taken it for parts.

A month before the inquiry was over, they called me: "Do you know about this piece of equipment?"

"Vaguely." I mean, I've shipped parts and equipment to six different continents.

I went down and testified. Anyway, they cut me off at the knees. In so many words, Eastern Health said my services would no longer be needed. Ninety per cent of my business was gone overnight. My options were limited, but I just happened to know the taxi industry. I know how to make a living at it; I haven't got to learn anything. Anyone who gets into this industry new does it because there's nothing else that they can do. For almost everybody who is over fifty or sixty, they're probably at it to supplement their income. You almost need to be on a pension, because sometimes you don't make minimum wage at this. I talked to a girl out in the Goulds at one of the local convenience stores. Her father is retired, and he went taxiing. About a month ago, he worked for nine hours on a Saturday and made $8. That's true. I've done it. Not recently, but I've done it.

Some people have no idea. Pick a Saturday or a Sunday morning when there's fuck all doing. How long are you prepared to sit in that car? Twelve hours in an average shift. We got eight or nine different places where we park: Knights of Columbus, Traveler's Inn, Stockwood's, the Quality Hotel, the Battery Hotel, Churchill Square, Cougar Helicopters, Stanley Steamer on Torbay Road, the trade schools. Workers' Compensation is another. We got small law firms. Stuff like that. You go find one of the stands to park at and hope that it gets busy. At any given time there are twenty-five to thirty-five cars on the road. If it doesn't get busy, you don't make any money.

What do you think is the longest shift I've ever worked? Twenty-eight hours without a break. My mortgage was due, and I never had it. I went to work until I got it. That's downright fucking dangerous. That's shit you shouldn't be at, but there are guys who do that on a regular basis.

Here it's quarter after seven in the evening. I've been up since five o'clock this morning. Someone could say to me right now, "Here's $800. Take me to Corner Brook." I'd be gone in a flash. Our stand rent is $335 a week. We pay our stand rent on Wednesdays. I got to pay them $335 tomorrow for stand rent. Today, this is a bad day. Right now, I've probably made $100 cash, including charges. Forty-seven dollars of that comes out for my stand rent. That leaves me with $53. I've got to put gas in the car. That's $10, or $15. That leaves me with $30. I smoke. I bought a pack of cigarettes today. You can't take sandwiches with you if you're out twelve or fifteen hours. It's just not practical. If you get a bite to eat, what are you left with when you get home? Not much.

Every year we got to bring our taxis down to get them inspected. You bring them to the garage, and then you bring them down to City Hall. The taxi inspector just makes sure you got all your paper work, that you got $1 million in liability on your insurance. He'll check out to make sure your signal lights are working. Just basic stuff. You've come from a garage and you've had your car inspected by a licensed mechanic. Then you pay the taxi inspector his $100 fee that goes to City Hall for your licence for a year.

There's just no end to the fees. There are fees for fucking everything. When I put this car on two-and-a-half years ago, it cost me $1,700. I had to pay it off before I put her on the road because you can't drive a taxi with a loan on it. The car company knows you're going to run that car down to the ground. So I had to take out a second mortgage to pay off the car and to pay off some other bills that allow me to go taxiing so I don't have too many bills racked up to the point where I can't make enough to live on. I had to get a meter and a sign installed: $700. My first insurance policy: $2,500. That had to be paid up front.

Then you're working all night and you get this asshole that jumps out of your car at two o'clock in the morning that owes you $50. If you're driving for someone else, you got to gas up. Now instead of making $250 for that busy night you're only making $200. Do you know what a "water haul" is? Ever see a fisherman haul up his net and there's fuck all in it? It's the same thing as going to somebody's house and nobody comes out. That's a water haul. If they send me to Mount Pearl, that's five bucks in gas and an hour out of my time wasted. You wait fifteen minutes because you want to make sure you're going to get your job. So you lost an hour on a busy Friday night, and you got $5 in gas burned. You get two or three of them in a night, and it'll ruin you. A typical Friday or Saturday night, you got $60 worth of gas gone, you bought a pack of smokes and something to eat because you've been working twelve hours. You got $70 left: $35 for the guy who owns the car, and $35 for yourself. You go home and say to the wife, "This is what I made."

She says, "Why are you doing this?"

"Because no one else will have me."

The other day, this lady got in the car. I got a rattle in the back. I know what it is. It's the sway-bar bushing. It can make an awful racket if you hit the right bump. Later that day, missus phoned in and complained down to the stand. The manager told me, "You're probably going to have to take your car off the road."

I called back. "Listen here, you get that lady who called. Tell her to pick the mechanic of her choice, and I'll get a full inspection done."

I don't drive a Cadillac, but I look after what I got. The thing about it is, if I lose a motor tomorrow I'm out of business. I can't afford to put a motor in the car. So then I got to go to work for somebody else. If that happens, I got to get another job because that isn't going to cut it. That person probably got two drivers on the car: a day driver and a night driver. The day driver wants to work certain hours, and the night driver wants to work certain hours.

A few months back, a guy in a truck ran up the side of my car. That was $4,000 worth of damage. Buddy struck me in an F-150 pickup truck just down the road here on O'Leary Avenue. He hit me—it was clearly his fault. He told me it was his fault: "Sorry about that. I wasn't looking." The passenger in the back heard what he said. I was stopped, he was going, and he hit me. My insurance company contacted his insurance company. You know what they said? I'm 100 per cent at fault. I'm taking him to small claims court. [*He points to a camera mounted on the dash.*] If I'd had that in my car at the time, I wouldn't have to prove a thing. Everything would have been on tape. It was the best $78 I've ever spent.

I put this car on the road the day after the Cameron Inquiry. That's two and a half years ago. Co-Op Taxi was the only stand that had an available licence. When I had the car on in 1997 or 1998 it was with Co-Op. If I wanted, I could leave here now and in a half an hour I'd have a taxi on at any of the stands in St. John's. Because I got the experience. But they're all alike. What's better, the devil you know or the devil you don't know? That's exactly the way it is.

Look, a lot of guys in the taxi industry, they're at it because they can't catch a break—for whatever reason. They're not necessarily illiterate; they probably got a good education. I mean, there's teachers and everything else that's after driving a taxi at one time or another. After the inquiry, I applied for fifty jobs. I'm probably the most experienced lab technician in the province—maybe in Canada—and I couldn't get a job. No one ever gave me a reason why they wouldn't hire me. I'm after taking stuff off of my resume. Can you believe that? I had to take stuff off of my fucking resume. It was either I had too much experience, or they thought I was looking for too much money, or because I was too old. I'm driving a taxi not because I want to but because I got to.

There Is No Life as a Taxi Driver

Brian, driving for four years

I was working for Newfoundland Farm Products Corporation as a plant manager. A year before they privatized the place they made my job redundant and put me out through the door.

I was eighteen months away from a full pension. Then, all of a sudden, I had nothing. I developed a stress disease. I went to my family doctor, and he said, "If you don't do something soon, you've got four to six months before you're in a box."

"Is that so?" I said. "You have a good day."

I left his office, went to the liquor store and bought a bottle of rum and started drinking.

My wife came home and said, "What's going on?"

I said, "Nothing. I'm just having a few drinks."

It was out of the normal because I never drank like that.

The next day, I got up, made a few phone calls, and went to work for AT & T Canada as a sales representative. I stayed at that for a few months, and then I went into business with Integrated Poultry Limited. They had just bought out Newfoundland Farm Products Corporation. IPL never lasted; they went under. But I knew that, anyway. Having been the plant manager down there, I knew right away what was going on. I knew the industry inside out. When they went under, Country Ribbon took it over. Because I was only there under contract, they got someone else to do the work I was doing for them.

When that finished, I went to work up in Alberta, did some training and came back home.

I knew Peter Gulliver, and I asked him if he was in need of any drivers. He said, "Sure. Come to work with us. No problem." I've been here ever since.

In order to make any money at this racket you got to work a lot of hours. I used to make $60,000 a year. I worked eight hours five days a week and made $60,000 a year with six weeks holidays. With taxiing, you got to work every day. You can't have weekends off because if you take weekends off you won't make enough money. You can come out here and work twelve hours and go home with $30 in your pocket. Whereas you can go downtown on a Friday or Saturday night and make ten times as much.

There is no life as a taxi driver. There is just no life. But you got to make a living. I usually come out around ten or eleven o'clock and I stay on until twelve or one in the morning. Last year, I started driving the school bus. I get up at seven o'clock and pick up the bus and start working. I could take off a day, or two days, or however many I want to take off, but then I got no salary coming in.

I was out of a job for thirteen months, and I had to use my pension in order to live. I had a mortgage and car payments. I had to draw on my pension to live. If I had left my pension alone, if I was able to, I'd have a pension today and I wouldn't have to be out taxiing. But I couldn't do that.

For me to get another job I would have to leave the province. At my age, I'm not going to do that. I'm fifty-seven. I'll be fifty-eight on my birthday. I'll be doing this for another little while, I guess—until my wife retires. Then I'll say to hell with it. Life's too short.

I'm Stuck at This
Steven, driving for eight years

I hurt my arm; I got repetitive strain. You can tell because I have to hold it up. It happened while I was working on an assembly line doing the same thing over and over again 5,000 times a day. For five and a half years, I did everything Workers' Compensation wanted me to do. Most people go down to the Miller Centre for six weeks. My treatments ended up lasting six months. I went down every day doing foolish stuff like walking up and down the hall with a wooden box in my arms. I took injections of cortisone and did hydrotherapy. Compensation classified me with what's called "permanent functional impairment." That got me $5,500 out of them. They give you the money because you're stuck with the injury for the rest of your life. But five grand is nothing. Then they offered me a taxi. I was like, "No, I don't want to go taxiing. I don't want to drive people around. Give me a little van for couriering."

"No, you can't do that," they said, "because you have to lift stuff."

I said, "That's not lifting. That's envelopes and small parcels."

It seemed to be the thing back then. People would say, "Go down and tell them you want a taxi. They'll buy you a car, or a van. Whatever you want." I guess it depends on how long you're on compensation and what your injury is. If you lost both of your legs, it's no good giving you a taxi.

Then they told me to get a job as a meter reader. She said, "You got ten weeks to get a job at it, or you're cut off."

I said, "A job with Newfoundland Power?"

"Yes, you got ten weeks."

I said, "My ducky, you need a letter from God to get a job with Newfoundland Power. I haven't worked in five and a half years. I wouldn't even hire me."

"If you think a letter from God will help, maybe you should get one." Those were her exact words.

I sold everything off, and me and the missus and the four kids moved to Ontario. I had no reason to go to Ontario. We were fine here; I was getting enough on compensation. I was Mr. Mom, and she was working. At least we had two incomes coming in. Then my wife had a nervous breakdown and came back to Newfoundland out of it. She never came back to me. I went painting cars for a little while. Then I went detailing cars—fancy cars. But you don't make a living at that when your rent is $1,200 a month. You're only getting $15 an hour. I said, "I got to get out of here. I don't care if I'm flipping burgers."

I phoned my buddy, and he said, "I'll get you a job taxiing."

I came back home, and I started at this. At first, I loved it. Then I liked it. Then I didn't mind it. Now I hate it. In a half an hour, I'll have eight hours punched in. As it is now, since four o'clock this morning, I haven't made fifty bucks, and that's everything on the meter. I'm working for about $3 an hour. Since four o'clock, I think I've had five jobs. That's it. I wouldn't recommend taxiing to an enemy, to be honest. It's the only job I know where you don't get stamps, you don't get compensation, and you don't get holidays, or sick leave. If you don't work, you don't get paid. I'm in a bind now. My rent was due last week. I had $120 for him yesterday, and the only reason I came up with that is because I went to Placentia for $285. I only have the use of one arm, and I can't do anything else. I'm stuck at this.

Just a Girl Driving a Taxi

Sandra, driving for four years

I used to work for an old answering service here in the city, the ones where you'd have to use the cord boards. If you called your oil company after ten o'clock at night you got one of us girls. Then we would call the oil man: "You got to deliver oil to old Mrs. Brown because she's froze down there." I think when I first started, they'd deliver $50 worth of oil. That'll tell you how long ago it was I worked there.

I was at the university for a spell doing clerical work. I would have loved to stay there and grow old in a little office. Absolutely. It's probably the healthiest environment I've ever worked in. Mentally, physically—everything. But it was just getting harder and harder to get contract jobs. That's how I was working, on a contract, and they didn't want to hire any more permanent positions. Nepotism, or whatever you call it, was getting more apparent, too.

On paper, I should've gotten this one job. I had more seniority. At that point, I had Mom home, too, and she wasn't healthy. I had Jimmy who I was trying to raise on my own. The importance of that job, and then not getting it, was absolutely devastating. I thought because you were supposed to get a job that you would get it. I guess somebody figured a girl living in a basement apartment on her own with no cares in the world deserved that job more than me. It was overwhelming, not getting that job, because it was so important to my future.

Three days later, the union called: "We need to talk to you. We think you should file a grievance. We think you got a really good case." But as grievances work, I didn't understand the process whatsoever. About a year or eighteen months later, I'm tortured to death. Everyone at my work thought I didn't want this young girl to have that job because I didn't like her. Through it all, I was the most unstable person ever. All you had to do was look at me, and I would cry. It was due to the bureaucracy of it all and the stress I had at home with Mom being sick. She'd had a couple of heart attacks, a stroke and the two knees done.

The last going off, the union said, "We have six really good grievance cases, but we're only going with two of them. Unfortunately, yours isn't one of them."

I was thinking, *Okay. What now?*

I got a meeting with the head of human resources. The main person with the union was off sick, and I got a replacement. The human resources guy started asking me all these personal questions. Of course, I'm welling up, and I answer them the only way I know how: "This job is important to me because I'm the healthiest person in my household. I've got my mom who is really sick, and I got a teenage boy home who I'm raising on my own."

He looked at me and said, "Do you need counselling? By the looks of it you need counselling. You're not very mentally healthy right now."

The whole meeting was an absolute nightmare.

In the midst of it all, a friend of mine commented, "My babysitter's father has got taxis. Why don't you give him a call if you need a job?"

I was just trying to find something temporary. I was looking at bars, and I didn't really want to go back to the bars. My son was going on a trip to St. Pierre, or Quebec, and I didn't have the money. He made a joke like a typical teenager: "You should get a job. You should drive a taxi."

In a matter of five days, I went from joking about it to being out in a taxi. I never had a clue how to taxi. The only thing the broker told me was that I couldn't wear jeans. He didn't give me a map book, he didn't give me anything like that. I was sent out on a Saturday morning. He told me who the dispatcher was. He told me that when I push the button on the radio to say car whatever and tell him where I was to. He drew all the stands out on a piece of paper. He sat in the car and held onto my finger like you would a child and pushed the buttons on the meter, he let it go, and he said, "Now you do it." Then he basically patted me on the arse and off I went.

I was frightened to death.

What surprised me was that I could never work another job and have the same level of money and availability as I do with taxiing. This week, I bought a couple extra things. I'll go to work tomorrow to pay for it. If I had something extra today, I'd go to work tonight. You make your money at your job, but how can you make more? Avon, maybe. Taxiing is the easiest way to have a job and a half. You don't even have to go home and change your outfit. I'd never have had that if I had stayed at the university.

Then there's the fact that it's easier to work with a bunch of guys. Say you got three female taxi drivers out on a night. Every time we're stopped waiting on a job it becomes a bitch fest. If you're dealing with the guys, you don't know if their mother's sick. You don't know if their wife is pregnant. You don't know that their youngster is on drugs. You don't know that their father just died. Whereas the minute you pull up to a female they'll tell you their life story.

It's the first time I've worked around this many men for this long. At the university, it was all women. We had just the one token male. It's so apparent that most guys don't have the same level of responsibility as women. Even the ones that do don't treat it the same. The ones who do take on responsibility still don't do it like a woman. There are a few whose daughters are on drugs, they got the baby, and they're struggling to pay all the bills. But they'll still drop everything on Wednesday to go get drunk. Whereas the females are like, "When am I going to be able to drop everything to go get drunk? Okay, I'll do it tomorrow." Then tomorrow becomes the next day, the next day become next week, and next week become next month.

At the stand, there's a group of the really old taxi drivers. They've got this ornery kind of way about them. They don't want to know your name, or your business. But they treated me differently because I'm a female. I could pull up to a stand, and they'd say, "Oh, did you hear? There's a few big jobs going out from here." They're not thinking that maybe I'll go and try to get it, or I'd remember it for next week. To them, I'm just a female—I don't threaten them. If I was a male driver they'd tell me where there weren't jobs. They'd send me in the wrong direction.

I guess I don't intimidate them; I don't scare them. That's how I got all the good bits of information when I first got started. Like I said to them, "I'm just a girl driving a taxi."

Poor-Mouthing

Margo, driving for six years

A lot of boys poor-mouth their way to tips. Their wife got her leg broke, and they're working extra hours. One of the kids wants a new bike but they don't have the money to buy it. One girl told the customers that she had a yeast infection. Can you believe that? I got a crowd of women in the car on the way back from downtown, and they said, "Oh, my god! We got another female driver."

I said, "Yeah, there's a few of us around."

"Are you going to tell us about your health problems? The other one told us she had a yeast infection. "

I went, "Oh, dear God!"

That made it funny because they knew I wasn't going to talk about any of my female issues, and I even got a tip afterwards. But it was probably on the back of the poor taxi driver who had the yeast infection. On the other side of it, I know what taxi driver that is. I'd like to go up to her and say, "What are you doing? Why are you discussing those issues with your customers? You're just making it harder on the rest of us."

I Need This Job

Max, driving for four months

The vast majority of St. John's taxicab drivers are from the Metro area. One driver said, "Years ago, there'd be a few scattered women around, but you'd be hard pressed to find a foreigner at it." There are indications that the number of immigrant taxicab drivers is rising, and their reasons for driving a cab seem remarkably similar to those of native Newfoundlanders. Still, many face additional obstacles such as language barriers and unusable foreign training, like this driver from the former Soviet Union.

For forty years, I live in Almaty. Almaty is first city of Kazakhstan. No problem for me before 1991. After 1991, when Kazakhstan separated from Russia, lots of criminals. You know, in Kazakhstan, there is lots of oil. When lots of oil, lots of money. When lots of money, lots of criminals. I'm an economist. I have a diploma in economics. In my country, I had a little business with two little stores. Criminal people want 50 per cent of what I make, and leave me with 50 per cent. If I don't give 50 per cent, this criminal people, they say, "I kill your family and fire your shops." They say come to my house and kill me, kill my son, kill my wife. I shake in terror. I sold my business, and I come here.

When I came to Canada, wife have divorce, and she live with my son in Calgary. I lived in Montreal for four months. In Montreal, very different people. I don't know why. In Montreal, lots of immigration people. Maybe this problem. I don't know. Here, if I not know, I ask you, I ask everybody. Everybody tell me, "Go here, go here, go here." In Montreal, if I ask everybody: "Ah, fuck you!" There are lots of languages in Montreal, lots of people—a very big city. I don't know French. I knew English a little bit.

I visited Toronto; I visited Ottawa. Very nice cities. In Toronto, in Ottawa, I don't know where I need go. I can't ask anybody. They say same as Montreal: "Fuck you! Fuck off!" I no ask because I know what they tell me.

My lawyer say, "Go to St. John's, Newfoundland." I come here, and I'm very happy here because one language and very good people. I like here because here easy. Not criminal. When I go to bed I no lock door. I know here not criminal. But my country, three or four locks.

St. John's has friendliest people. Very good people.

My diploma not good here because economics Russia, economics Kazakhstan and economics Canada very different. My diploma here not good. First time, I work dishwasher. After I buy car, I work pizza store delivery driver. Five years. Here driving taxi I only work three or four months.

I have experience from when I work in pizza store. Every time I use my map when I first start working. I study, study, study map. Now I know city. Sometimes, I no understand speaking. My English not good. Sometimes I no understand where I need go. If I no understand, customer write me—I check, I read. No problem. I know this street, I know this avenue, I know this road. I understand maybe 75 per cent. If no understand, I ask again. If no understand, customer show me where I need drive.

I like taxiing but it very difficult for me. I work many hours. I understand I need money. I need to work ten, twelve hours in day. I tired. I know this not good for me. I need rest. Here I can't take food because sitting. Every time I sit here in the car. Sometimes long times, sometimes short times in this car waiting for customer.

In St. John's, not lots of jobs. I need this job.

A Bunch of Cutthroats

Danny, driving for three years

While tipping, meaning "to give gratuity," can be traced to the Middle Ages, its modern origins come from eighteenth century Europe. In the post-Civil War era, wealthy Americans traveling through Europe brought the practice home with them to demonstrate their worldliness and sophistication. Tipping soon became widespread. In coffee houses and pubs, signs reading "to insure promptitude" adorned prominently placed containers.

Some social scientists point out that tips are an expression of empathy for workers who earn low wages. The expectation of a tip complicates the relationship between taxicab drivers and their customers. Historically, the practice of tipping brought taxicab drivers closer to what might be best described as "service workers." While taxicab drivers might reject the characterization, according to historian Graham Hodges, "Their relationships with customers and the chase for better tips make them resemble servants."

There are good tippers, there are stern tippers, and there are bad tippers. The stern tippers are the type of people who let you know that they're giving you a dollar. The university crowd, the younger crowd, don't know the meaning of a tip. They're the bad tippers. You'd be lucky to get an extra nickel out of them. Then there are the freeloaders. If you're close, the meter is negotiable. If you got eight bucks and the meter says ten, then eight is fine. But don't do it every weekend. I'm out; I'll recognize you. What are you supposed to do with them? We got guys on the stand that if you don't have the fare right to the meter they'll take you straight to the RNC.

But drivers know that the cops don't want to charge them. The cops are like, "Come on. Is it necessary for us to charge this person?"

"Hang on now. What if you got paid $22 for an eight hour shift? What if you got paid $5 for the first hour you punched in? How does that sound?"

I drove a couple to Oxen Pond Road this past weekend. It came to twelve bucks. They only had eight. I was being nice, and I said, "Eight bucks is good. Don't worry about it."

She got out, and the guy got out. They had a kiss and said their goodbyes. She went on, and buddy got back in.

I said, "Where are we going, bud?"

"Higgin's Line."

It hit me that they didn't have enough money to begin with. "Do you have any money?"

"No."

"I can't drive you to Higgin's Line with no money, man."

Of course, he was a young university student. He was like, "Come on."

"I'm out here working," I said. "This pays my bills and buys my groceries. It keeps my heat and light on."

I don't understand a lot of the younger people. They all work in the service industry; they're all waitresses and waiters and bartenders and bouncers. But still and all they don't tip, and half the time they don't even have enough to cover the fare. A tip is everything, especially for a cab driver.

It's got nothing to do with how much money they make, either, or how much they got in the bank. I think it comes down to ignorance. Some people got everything given to them, I guess, and never know what it's like to work for a living. The people you know who got nothing are the ones who usually do try to give you something extra. They know what it's like being out trying to make a dollar.

This elderly couple were going from the Quality Inn to Bacalao there on LeMarchant Road. It was a $7 run. I came straight across Duckworth Street, up over Barter's Hill and right on LeMarchant

Road. The man said, "We didn't come this way last time. We went through Rawlin's Cross."

"I didn't want you to have to cross the street in traffic. I wanted to let you off on the right side of the road."

"I'm sure now," he said. His voice and his demeanour was pretty condescending. "You just wanted a few extra dollars in your pocket."

I tried to be polite. "No, sir. I'm not ripping you off. On a small run like this I'm not going to rip you off for twenty-odd cents. I mean, come on."

His wife was telling him to give it up. But he kept on and kept on.

In the meantime, while he was telling his wife that he was in the right, I turned the meter off. He stopped the conversation. "Why did you turn the meter off?"

I said, "If $7 is going to be out of the way for you and your woman to have a good night out, then the ride is for free. You got me feeling bad over $7, man. Go out to dinner, and go have a good time. Don't worry about it."

He was like, "Yes, right on!"

But his wife was good and pissed off. She gave me a $3 tip. When they walked away, she said everything to buddy: "Why do you have to do that every single time? Every single time you hassle cab drivers."

I drove an old guy out to Petty Harbour. He had this sandy, sandpaper face. He was big, too. He was six-four, or six-five—a big old fisherman. All the way out, he was tearing me a new asshole: "Cab drivers are all a bunch of cutthroats. I suppose I got to pay forty bucks now for this run. For fuck sake, I wouldn't burn $3 in gas driving home in my truck."

You don't usually comment too much. But I said, "You can walk, or you can get caught for impaired driving. That's six or seven grand and your licence gone."

When he got out, I happened to look back, and I noticed that he dropped his money on the seat. It was at least three grand worth of fifties. It was a big old stack of them. I was new to the business and young. Being raised the way I was raised, I gave him back his money hoping to change his perspective on cab drivers. That would've made my day. I got out with the money, and said, "Hey, buddy. Come here, I want you."

He turned around, and I stuck out my hand. He said, "I'm not shaking your hand, you cutthroat."

"Look closer."

And there was his money in my hand. He took his money and said, "You're all still a bunch of cutthroats."

If You Want to Drive, Get Your Own Cab

Gordon, driving for eighteen years

Some customers think they can get away with anything. They get in the car and they think they own it. I remember one of the other drivers, a good buddy of mine, had someone burn cigarette holes in his back seats. The driver told the passenger he couldn't smoke in the car, and he took the plastic knobs off of the locks and twisted the steel. I had one guy reach over, drunk, and try to take control of the steering wheel. I had to hit him with an elbow in the forehead. This was a big guy, too, biceps like footballs. Going down Craigmiller Avenue, he reached over the seat and grabbed the steering wheel. There were cars on both sides of the road and children playing.

I said, "Listen, buddy, I'm driving this taxi. If you want to drive, you get your own car. I'm damn well sure that if a youngster comes out from between two cars and gets hit, your story isn't going to be the same as mine."

Then I had another guy who, oddly enough, I picked up at a cab driver's house. It's early on a Friday night—it's not even dark out—and he's drunk. I said, "Where are you headed?"

He told me to take him to the east end of town, behind the Holiday Inn—around that way. He then reached over turned the meter off. "You don't need that on," he said.

"As a matter of fact, I do. I got a family to feed, bud. I don't know where you get off."

Then he turned the meter off again. He said, "You don't need that on."

"As a matter of fact, I do. And don't touch it again."

"Buddy, I got to make a phone call."

I knew there was going to be a dozen stops, and I knew I probably wouldn't get paid. I brought him to the Fountain Spray on Military Road. It's a Needs Store now. I decided to just drive away and leave him there. That's the best thing to do with those kinds of guys.

Have a Nice Day, My Darling

Fitz, driving for fifteen years

I picked her up this missus at the airport, took her luggage and got her aboard. You know—common courtesy stuff. Everything went number one. I brought her down to her place, and she paid me for the job right to the penny. We're responsible to put whatever they need a hand with on their step, so I haul her bags out of the back of the car. There was no tip, or nothing. "Follow me," she said.

"Excuse me?"

"I want you to bring them upstairs for me."

I looked at her: "Bring them upstairs for you? Do you want me to unpack them and put them back in the drawers, too?"

"Don't you get smart with me," she said, "or I'll call and complain."

I wasn't having that. "I hope you do. Have a nice day, my darling."

She started in again: "I demand…"

You try to humour them and do the best you can, but sometimes you get fed up. "You demand what? For me to go upstairs and for me to take your luggage and put it in your bedroom? You're cracked, girl. What's wrong with your head?"

What it All Boils Down To

Don, driving for twenty-two years

The thing about St. John's is we're now on par with the national average of unemployment, which is five-point-something. The city is doing well. We got more people working. We got the university. We got five major hotels. There's money out there. But yet they'll be into the restaurants and into the bars and when it comes time to go home in a taxi they want a cut rate. I've seen them walk from car to car to car down Adelaide Street looking for a deal.

With me, the meter goes on—that's it.

That being said, if I give you my cell number you can phone me for a taxi. But the difference with me is I won't personalize company work. That work is for everyone. I'll take the jobs in turn. Guys used to come in off the rigs to get their checks and give me a call. There used to be four coming in one week and four the next. I drove them around, and I told them if they wanted cigarettes or booze picked up, I'd do that, too. There was always a good tip because they had a pocket full of cash. After a few weeks, one of them might say, "Don, can I owe you $20 until we get back?" That stuff didn't bother me; I was doing pretty well for myself.

Then you got customers who call three or four taxis at a time and whoever gets there first gets the job. It happens too often. But we just sit back and take it.

My last New Year's Eve was four years ago. They were out on the streets and up at the hotels. It was busy everywhere. I dropped someone off in Kilbride at quarter to four in the morning, and the dispatcher fed me another job in the same area. When I got them to Forest Road—downtown was just over the hill, seconds away— the customer said, "Did you get a call from up there? I called five or six cabs."

"Why didn't you tell me that earlier?" I said. "I'd have left you right where you were to. Would you phone for five or six pizzas and just pay for the one that got their first?"

He didn't like that. But I didn't like what he said to me, either.

And it's mostly the younger crowd—students. I'm not saying it's always students. I'm just saying they're usually young. One time, I got sent to Burton's Pond, the university. They were in the back seat on the phone, and one of them said, "Can you cancel that cab?"

I pulled the car off the road: "Get out! Next time you won't be so smart."

I've often had instances where another driver and I got to a house at the same time and we left them right where they were to. But you got drivers out there who don't care, as long as they can get that job. We got to stand up for ourselves. Phoning three or four taxis is not right.

It all boils down to the fact that there's no respect—you're not even looked at. You're nothing. That's the way I feel. I once watched a guy on *Good Morning America* interview a hot dog vendor on Park Avenue. You can imagine what it's like having a hot dog stand on Park Avenue. Just before the interview was over, the vendor said, "I guess other than taxi drivers we're looked down upon."

The Nature of the Business

Doug, drove and dispatched for twenty-five years

Most cab drivers are eager to tell their stories to complete strangers—customers—but once a microphone is turned on they generally go quiet. But consider that many of their work-related experiences centre on other drivers, as well as the owners, the brokers, sometimes the police and often City Hall. There are the drivers who rob jobs from other drivers. The inspectors who do little inspecting and a lot less enforcing. The stand owners who put junkers on the road and nutbars behind the wheel. Some drivers simply fear retaliation. One, bold and brash, laughed: "It certainly wouldn't be the first time someone got a punch in the face for mouthing off."

I liked my job and the people I worked with, and the dispatchers got treated with respect. But, after twenty-five years, I got sick of babysitting children. Last going off, I used to come in and announce over the radio, "All right, boys. I'm here and I've only got half a case of Pablum and six pacifiers. Go easy on me."

Drivers were removing customers from other cars and putting them in their own car because they felt they were supposed to get that particular job. Drivers were racing to get ahead of other cars and cutting them off so they could pull up in front of the house first. Drivers were calling and forever lying about where they were to. If they were quick enough to click in before the one-and-three-quarter seconds it took the other guy to respond, even if they're camped out in a line-up at one of the stands, they'd put on the reverse lights, back away and nobody would be the wiser. Drivers were going flat out down over the hill and calling their buddies on the radio to pull over, they got to ask them something, and then zooming on past them to get to a job. It got to be too much for me.

It wasn't hard to figure out someone was lying. If you just left the stand for a job, and I had your name crossed off, there was no way you were ready for another job halfway across town. There was no way you got from Adelaide Street to the Janeway, dropped off your job and were parked at Virginia Park Plaza, which was the standby stand, and were ready for another job that quick. It's impossible. I knew they were full of shit; everyone on the stand knew they were full of shit.

Our radio sets used to be closed—you could only hear the dispatcher, and you couldn't hear the other drivers. This was before cellphones. When the open microphone system was introduced it kept people honest and got rid of a lot of the garbage going out over the system.

One guy—I won't name no names—was a prime example of the way things used to be. He was a poster child for screwing over the dispatchers and customers. He was an intimidator, a former drug dealer who had done a string of time and whose choice of career when he got out of jail was taxiing. Taxi intimidation, more like it. He'd cut you off on the road, or rob a job right in front of you. Shit like that. A few times he told me he was going to come down and throw me out the window for giving one of his jobs to another driver.

I guess I was starting to piss some people off.

I was calling out the bullshitters: *You just had a job and you want another?* If one guy was a flat-out liar and the other a career driver, I knew who was telling the truth. Greed—that's what it's all about. But that's the nature of the business.

Sky Pilots

Paul, driving and dispatching for seventeen years

You must've heard of "sky pilots." Those are the drivers who you haven't heard from for hours, guys who won't work with the dispatcher the whole night, and all of a sudden they answer the radio at four in the morning when downtown is cleaned up and they're looking for phone work. It's like they appear out of nowhere. But you know they've been on the go the whole night. You've watched them out the window as they blow by. You'll radio into the dispatcher to let them know what they're at, cruising around and not taking jobs off the phone. Then you'll hear: "Forty-two? I hope you're listening, because you're not getting anything from me after four o'clock."

I prefer to work with the dispatcher. If I'm in the area and he wants a car, I'll call out. I'll tell you now, I was in on Brookfield Road and the dispatcher whacked me to the Fairview Inn. You mean to tell me there were no other cars between me and the east end? You let out your dirty digs—your complaints. The dispatcher knows you're frustrated, but what can he really do about it?

When I dispatched, with that many drivers out there, when I came in at eleven-thirty, I put my foot down: "If you don't work with me now, come four o'clock in the morning you're not getting anything off the phone." I'd say that in order to get the drivers to work with me because the company got regular customers waiting. Those same regulars are going to be there Monday, Tuesday, Wednesday and Thursday when there's nothing doing. You got to try to keep them happy.

The Downtown Rush

Donald, driving and dispatching for seventeen years

Some of the brokers are pretty tight. On average, if you drove 100 kilometres you should have about $35 for them. But see I'm a cruiser. I cruise. So if you expect $35 out of me and I'm cruising around and I'm not getting no work and I put on twenty or twenty-five kilometres before I get a job for only a run up over the hill and you expects $35 then you're cracked. I give them half of what's on the meter. My tips are my own.

For me, if you expect that $35 for every 100 kilometres, I'll give him back the keys. You can drive me back home. I'm at it long enough, and they all know me. I'll work my twelve hours. I know that at the tail end of my shift, at the ninth and tenth hour, when these weekend warriors are gone home, there's that three hour window when there's only a few cars on the streets. You're flat out then. You can make sixty, seventy, eighty or ninety bucks just cruising. All you got to do is take one from downtown and head out over the overpass with them, and that's $40 there.

But I can see where the owners are coming from. The price of everything has gone up. If you go 100 kilometres, you should have $100 on your meter. But then you take twenty for gas, and that leaves you with eighty. Then you split that, and that's forty. You're coming into an average of $35 each. Let's say, for argument's sake, a broker has got fifteen cars available for Friday and Saturday night. For fifteen cars, he got seventeen drivers for Friday night. Two of them got to do without a car. The bottom two, to my knowledge, that made the least amount of money on Friday night won't get a car on Saturday.

The real difficulty is starting off in the early part of the night. Since the bars changed their hours from two o'clock until three o'-clock they shot themselves in the foot. Most people, students, used to rush home, get cleaned up and rush downtown. Now they party until twelve o'clock, and then they get the taxi downtown. They got that extra hour. You got three hours of drinking; they're priming up at home. What is it, $6 a beer down there now? Look at the George Street Festival. That's gone retarded. Thirty bucks to get in on the street. When I first started out, I used to drive my brother's car from six or seven o'clock until six or seven in the morning. There used to be seven of us out there, seven drivers. We used to be that busy that we had enough work to keep us going the whole night. Now you're sitting around waiting until around midnight before you really get going.

A Vicious Cycle
Allen, driving for twenty-two years

Before the bars close, downtown is not phone work. I cruise Water Street and Duckworth Street, and I'll shoot up Adelaide and look for a job. We used to tell the regular customers to go up by Mile One if they're heading west or to go up by Club One if they're heading east. You drive up and lock your doors, and people start swarming your car. Then the customer you're there to pick up might only be going up to Gear Street. But that person is a regular customer, and that's what they called us for, a run up the hill for $5.

Then you get others: "Thanks for picking me up. Take me to Mount Pearl for fifteen?"

"No way. How'd you get downtown?"

"Valley Cabs."

"You can pay what's on the meter, or you can get out in the cold and wait for Valley Cabs."

Out-of-town taxis aren't supposed to be down there. That's the regulation. But still and all taxis from CBS are down there taking work. Taxis from Paradise are down there taking work. What's a taxi from CBS doing down in Logy Bay Road? We're not allowed to pick up and drop off in Mount Pearl or Paradise. We're not allowed to pick up in Mount Pearl and drop off in St. John's. But we're allowed to pick up downtown and drop them off in Mount Pearl.

If those cabs are going to be at it, I got no problem doing the same. It's like a vicious cycle. When I do pick up someone in Mount

Pearl, I'll haul into somewhere like Tol's Time Out Lounge. Buddy might get in the car, and I'll take him wherever he wants to go. If I see a cop around, I shut off the meter and just say, just like everyone else does, "You're related to me."

Make the Most of What You Got

Leonard, driving for four years

People can't afford to go out and buy new taxis. You got to make the most of what you got. You're not making enough money, and what you got is worked to death. If you see an old car that used to be a taxi stay away from it because that car is worn out and isn't fit to be on the road. If someone reports it the city got to do something about it. But other than that, there's only so many random inspections that they can get around to. That's another problem you can't fix with the number of people they got down there. I'll tell you this. If there are 100 taxis out there I'd say eighty of them shouldn't be on the road.

Cribbing

Sandra, driving for four years

You can make a decent living at this. It's just a matter of how you handle your money. This job changes how you prioritize. When I was getting paid once every two weeks, the day after I got paid I'd probably go get a case of beer and a little draw. That'd do me for however long. It's different now. Pot becomes a priority. I pack a lunch and make sure I got change for a coffee. I'll smoke a draw before I go, and I'll roll one for later on when I have to pull over because I'm ready to snap.

I can't say I speak for all of them, but about 80 per cent of the drivers I know smoke pot. They all got the same kind of mindset. It's one o'clock in the morning. All the customers are getting on my nerves. I'll go have a break and smoke a joint. Then the rest of the night is way easier to deal with.

You smoke more cigarettes, you drink more coffee and you eat take-out. So if you weren't doing that and you worked five days a week you could easily take in about $600 cash. But if you're taking in $600, that's not what you're giving the boss.

With the guy I drive for, he wants half of what's on my meter, and he wants me to turn on the meter as much as possible. But he expects that at the end of the night he'll see a few more kilometres than I have money. With some brokers they want you to pay a dollar and a quarter a kilometre. If I got $400, I should have about 330 kilometres. That's why when somebody asks if you can take them to Mount Pearl for $20 you take the $20. What the boss doesn't know won't hurt him. It's called "cribbing," working off the meter.

One time, I didn't have the right kilometres. The boss said, "You're cribbing me!"

I said, "What?"

"You don't know what cribbing is?"

He assumed I didn't and went into great detail about how it's robbing and how you go about doing it. He gave me about twenty ideas on how to do it. "Now that you know that I know," he said, "you better not be at it."

But you do it according to the broker you drive for. There are some brokers that I won't drive for because I'd make less money. I just got too much respect for them. I wouldn't be able to do what I can do with another broker who might've pissed me off.

Costing Regular Business
Allen, driving for twenty-two years

For years, while the taxi inspector was there, nobody shagged around. If you had to go see the taxi inspector, if somebody made a complaint about you, he'd sit you down, and it made you pretty nervous. People had a lot of respect for him—a little bit of fear and a lot of respect—because he kept you on your toes.

The last time the city had a full-time taxi inspector down there was probably in the early '90s. He was doing a good job, too. He'd be down there on a Friday night looking for cars with defects, cars that didn't have working lights and proper stickers. Stuff like that. Sometimes these big stand owners have cars floating around without proper stickers on them. The stand owner might have an extra car and an extra driver. They just stick a radio in a car and send them out. It's not legal, but the stand owner might say, "Go on and take it. Make an extra couple bucks for the weekend." The taxi inspector had the power to stop that sort of stuff. He'd stand up on the corner of Adelaide Street and George Street and haul people off the road. If you got too many people in your car, he'd go over and issue a citation. A lot of that is on the go. There might be six or seven students heading home from downtown that'll pile up in the car: "We'll give you two bucks each to take us to the university." But you're not supposed to take any more than four or five passengers. If you have an accident, you're not insured. The insurance won't cover you because you got too many people in the car.

There are a lot of junkers out there, too. They're only inspected by City Hall once a year. That inspection is pretty perfunctory. All they do is check the signal lights, headlights, and backup lights. They check to see if your doors open. They don't take it off the road and lift it up on the ramp.

The taxi inspector was there to prevent things like that from happening. These days, if the city needs someone to do something like an inspection someone comes over from Housing.

It seemed like we had a little bit more legitimacy when there was a taxi inspector. You had somebody to answer to. Now it's like any fool can drive a taxi. We got guys coming from Ontario and British Columbia thinking there's this big job market here and then they can't find anything. What do they do? They go drive a taxi. They're out there driving and they don't know where they're going. It's costing us regular business. The funniest one I ever heard was when I was working at Gulliver's. The taxi stand is on Adelaide Street, right in front of City Hall. The dispatcher called out, "Car such and such head over to the front of City Hall."

Buddy radios back: "Where's that to?"

They Got to Get These Cars Moving

Gordon, driving for eighteen years

Over the past thirty years, the city has slowly deregulated the process of monitoring who could operate a taxicab. Starting in 1976, under Section 16 of the Taxicab Bylaw, part-time drivers were permitted. Soon after, City Council amended the bylaw by removing the "sole occupation" restriction which permitted part-time taxi drivers, but only if it was their sole occupation. In a memorandum to the city, the taxicab inspector raised his concerns that, because of the change, full-time drivers might suffer a loss of income. But many of the part-time drivers who entered the industry worked shifts the career drivers were unwilling to accept, mainly those at night.

To get a taxicab driver's licence, drivers were once required to present a letter of conduct from the Royal Newfoundland Constabulary. But, starting in 2000, the city dropped the regulation in favour of self-regulation, or owner operators, brokers and stand owners monitoring the quality of their drivers. In an editorial to The Telegram *entitled "Know Who's Driving Your Cab? Neither Does the City," one concerned driver stated, "The stand owners are under no onus to ensure a review of the driver's past performance, or that it excludes criminal behaviours that may put passengers at risk."*

I didn't like it from the first day I started, right up until now. But this province has got fuck all to offer you. I tried to get out of it a couple of times, but you know what they say about taxiing, that you'll always come back to it. No hard labour, or nothing. The industry isn't fit for human consumption. There's nothing straight about the owners. The drivers are dirtbags, people on welfare. Some of the lowest forms of life are driving taxis. There's no money at it, but combined with what they make on their welfare check, by the time they give buddy who owns the car half they're probably making $500 a week. There are a few well-to-do people out there. There are retired people at it. But when a taxi hauls up to your door you don't know what you're going to get. The driver could be the lowest form of criminal in this city, or he could be the most respectable man you've ever met. You just don't know.

The owners got to get these cars moving. They got to get people in them. If it comes down to hiring mental patients, they don't care. There's even talk that they used to go down to the penitentiary and wait for drivers to get out from doing weekends and put them to work. You can't get a good man at it no more, a good respectable man, because there's not enough money to be made for a good respectable man to go out there. What good respectable man is going to go out and put in eleven hours to come home with fifty bucks? What happens is you get the shady people driving taxis: welfare recipients, drug dealers, people who never worked a day in their goddamn life. There are a lot of investors in at it now, too, guys who own other businesses. We call them "fleeters." They don't drive the taxis. They just sit home while another bunch is out paying for the gas to keep them on the road. The cars are complete junk. They don't care what happens to nothing.

The government doesn't know they're out taxiing. The drivers don't say they're working, and it's all cash money. I guess unemployment doesn't give a damn, and the same goes for welfare. I phoned down, and they said, "Buddy, there's nothing we can do about that. We don't have the manpower. You're only wasting your time calling us."

Let's face it. We're in St. John's, man. What's out there? There's nothing here—nothing. There's lots of welfare. They say that for every dollar we give Ottawa, Ottawa gives us four back, and that's in welfare and unemployment checks. When you're out driving a taxi, on the fifteenth of the month and the thirtieth of the month the city comes alive. Your phone rings off the hook because the welfare people are out getting their groceries.

The tourists who come down from Toronto say, "I heard so much about your city." The next thing, they get in the back of a cab and they're doing 130 kilometres. Buddy is probably after smoking three joints, he's on welfare, and he's probably after drinking a flask before he even came to work. It's going on. It's going on because that's the only people they can get to drive the taxis. If there was money out there to be made and the city could properly regulate the taxi business, the nice sensible man might want to hand his business on down to his son. Then you might not have these nutbars flying around. But that's all that's out there—retards.

There are saner people incarcerated in the Waterford Hospital. I'm telling you there are saner people in the Waterford Hospital. I can take you to three drivers, right now. They work every night. They're like robots, mechanically inclined robots. They work every night of the week. And they're gone. [*Points to his temple; his hand is shaped like a pistol.*] It reflects back on the city. This is the city's image. I've heard instances where people will pass the Basilica, and they ask, "What year was that built?"

Buddy will say, "How the fuck do I know when it was built?"

The city is hurting.

No one can do anything about it. What can they do? The city, these fools who sit around the table on Channel 9, they don't know what to do. *This Hour Has 22 Minutes* is better than those fools. They don't know what to do. They make one wrong move and these stand owners will sue their asses. The big boys are too powerful, and they're afraid of them.

They could buy back some licences, or something. There's 364 taxi licences out there. This city is only big enough for 250, maybe. If the owners could get another ten licences off City Hall tomorrow they'd have them. They don't care about the driver. The driver is dirt. "You piece of dirt, get out there and make fifty bucks. You bring me back fifty bucks, or you won't get a car for the weekend."

No one knows how to fight the big stand owners. They're too powerful. They're multi-millionaires.

The Last Time We Got a Raise

Paul, driving and dispatching for seventeen years
In the highly competitive taxi industry, cab drivers rarely show unity. But disunity isn't an insurmountable obstacle. When the 15 per cent harmonized sales tax went into effect on April 1, 1997, the city dragged its feet in adjusting the Taxi Bylaw. For weeks, taxi meters read 7 per cent, while drivers covered the additional 8 per cent. One driver echoed the frustrations over how City Council had handled the increase: "The whole bloody bunch has taken leave of their senses." When their anger finally spilled over, it led to a massive mid-day protest. In what The Evening Telegram *described as "an unusual show of solidarity," over 100 cabs from several companies blocked off the west-bound lanes of New Gower Street directly in front of City Hall. An emergency meeting was immediately held between industry representatives and the mayor. A day later, taxi fares were increased to offset the tax increase.*

Every union in this city, including City Hall who got the say of what happens with taxis, always got three and four-year contracts. Raises were 4, 8 and 12 per cent. If a union in St. John's wants a raise and doesn't get it, what do they do? They go out on strike. The last time the taxi industry got a raise was four years ago. The time before that was ten or fifteen years ago when all the taxis cried foul. Nobody listened, and we parked 100 cars in front of City Hall. I was one of them.

A Peaceful Demonstration
Mark, driving for twenty-one years

Supposedly, the big stand in town got a permit to go up Adelaide, right across from George Street, whereas the rest of us taxicab companies got to go around the corner and park and wait for a run. That one stand is only supposed to have four cars on Adelaide at any one time. The other taxis have to park around the corner.

I don't know the rights of it, but why is one taxi company allowed an unfair advantage over the others? On Regatta day, you got a lot of people who want to take a taxi home, people who are tired, people who are old, and people with kids. Why is it that our stand can't have access to King's Bridge Cabs? The city won't allow it—that's why. They got it blocked off. Over the years, when I worked the Regatta, I used to go down King's Bridge Road, turn left onto Empire Avenue and wait on the corner. We all used to do it. They cut us out from going down there because they brought the buses in. That's City Hall interfering with the buses again, putting them in so they can make money. It's the same thing with the cruise ships. The city will haul all the buses down and load them up, and we're left with the scraps.

We organized a committee in order to stop the way things were run, and the superintendent of the police department came down to speak with us. He said, "We'll let you have a peaceful demonstration to get your point across." He had us head east on Water, turn left onto Adelaide, and then loop around. There had to be close to 200 cars that came down, and there's only 364 in this city. That'll tell you the kind of support we got.

We wanted to try to get different things changed to make it fair for everybody. But they had their minds made up before we went down. One evening, they started off with their usual bullshit, and a guy I know—he's very quiet, like a mouse—opened his mouth. Out of all the meetings, he finally had enough and told the Director of City Engineering right where to go. He said, "You're nothing but a liar!"

Fighting Over Scraps
Charlie, driving for thirty-seven years

Among taxicab drivers, the most commonly expressed misconceptions about the taxicab industry are that the licence holders (stand owners, brokers and owner operators) own their taxicab licences and that there are too many taxicabs operating in St. John's. These are beliefs born out of the frustration of not being able to affect positive change. Historians call this "revisionism." In the case of the St. John's taxicab industry it is a reordering of the past which serves the function of explaining oppression and exploitation.

In reality, unlike New York, where taxicab drivers purchase "medallions" at exorbitant prices, in St. John's, the city leases licences. Researchers working on behalf of the Commission of Inquiry into the St. John's Taxicab Industry combed the mountain of documentation in the city's archives. Beginning in 1989, all cabs were required to be attached to a stand. During the inquiry, some stand owners stated that prior to the change in regulation they held the operator licence. But because of this arbitrary decision by council, the licences were given to the drivers. However, the commission determined that "before 1989, applications for a stand licence were taken by the stand owners to mean taxicab operator licences. But the bylaw was quite clear. The stand did not acquire these. The cab owners did." Commission researchers also examined the number of taxicabs operating in other similarly sized cities as St. John's: Halifax, Dartmouth, Saint John, Kitchener-Waterloo and Hamilton. They determined that St. John's had a comparable number of taxis offering an adequate level of service. In fact, St. John's consistently ranks below the national average of taxis per-capita. But the belief that the stand owners hold the licences, and that these licences are too numerous, persists.

Somebody needs to do a survey across Canada to find out how many taxis should be on the streets in a city like ours. We probably got twice the national average. Anytime somebody retires and got a licence, retire the licence. We got 364 taxis in St. John's. In 1980-

something, we had 364 taxis in St. John's. And there was no business then, either. But now we got 364 taxis with about 2,000 drivers. But back then you had 364 taxis and 1,000 drivers. The only thing that's going to correct this industry is to pick a number that sits well with how much population there is. If you got 500,000 people, pick a number. Right now, the number of taxi licences that are given out each year are based on arbitrary numbers. The numbers are random, at best.

There's a whole story behind that. It was the late '80s, or the early '90s. I don't remember the exact time. All the individual taxi companies owned the licences. For instance, Dave Gulliver, who owned Gulliver's Taxi, he probably had forty or fifty licences. A lot of people in the taxi industry didn't like the owners having all the licences. They spoke up and said, "We think the individual drivers should own the licences."

There was a lot of spitting and shitting and, within a couple of years, City Hall said, "Fuck it!" They revoked all the licences, or something to that effect. If you're driving the car for a year and you owned that car, you now owned the licence that's on the side of your sticker. For instance, if a company like Gulliver's had fifty cars—I don't know if that's accurate or not, but it was up there—those licences were divided down the middle somehow. There were 364 taxis in St. John's, and 170 thereabouts were still owned by the stands. The other 170 were owned by the drivers.

When these guys retire, most times, one of the large companies will buy the licence and put a car on. Two years before most guys pack it up, they've got a buyer. It shouldn't be. Those licences should be retired because there are too many taxis in St. John's. That's why nobody can make a living at it.

Saturday and Sunday afternoon there won't be much business. If it's like this week, there won't be nothing doing, I mean nothing—this is as bad as it gets. We got the May 24th weekend coming up. I like to go fishing. I can't. I got to work on Saturday. Guess who else will be working on Saturday? The rest of the brokers who made fuck all during the week. They're compounding the problem. Instead of ten cars working on Saturday you got twenty. They got to work. Do you see what I'm saying?

Go to PEI, Charlottetown, for instance, which, I guess, is the largest city in PEI, and ask them how much they're making taxiing. Those guys are over there making a damn good living. How do I know that? I drove them in my car when they came to the airport in St. John's. They were going on vacation like everybody else. When I asked them what they were making, I was flabbergasted. It was something like four times what we're making.

For the first time in eons, our population is starting to creep up just a little tiny bit. Over the last thirty years, it was constantly going down, but the number of taxis stayed the same. It's constantly going down because people are moving away. The rest are staying and can't get a job at anything else. Guess what they're going at? Driving a taxi. Taxis are full with drivers, but they're not full with passengers.

During the early part of the last century, cab men operated an automobile in the summer and a horse and side-sled in the winter. They most often went to the harbour or railway station on the east end of Water Street looking for a "hobble," or casual work.

With the outset of WWII, some companies, like Burgess Brothers' Cabs, took the opportunity to expand their business by building a garage to service their taxicabs, common practice amongst taxi fleets in larger North American cities.

Courtesy of Roy Burgess

Parked in his son's garage is Roy Burgess' first car, a '38 Nash. A taxicab sign is still attached to the roof, the original fare meter still in the glove box. "She's the only antique taxicab in this city," he said.

Courtesy of Roy Burgess

The city was playing catch-up to a swiftly urbanizing society when it passed the "Taxi Bylaw" in November 1950, adapting existing regulations to meet technological advancements and an increased demand for service. The bylaw made annual taxi driver licences manditory and set minimum employment standards for drivers.

During WWII, with the influx of thousand of Allied troops, taxi stands began to pop up seemingly overnight. Some, like Snow's Taxi on Pearce Avenue and Star Taxi, were operated from dispatch offices in backyard sheds.

In 1946, Frank O'Keefe opened O.K. Taxi on George Street. Many men who had experience taxiing prior to the war returned to the one job where they knew they could make a dollar: taxiing.

Many taxicab operators had what was referred to in the 1950 "Taxi Bylaw" as a "taxi man's shelter," a place where they could "escape the elements."

Pressured by high insurance premiums and other exorbitant start-up costs, few taxicab drivers buy new cars and many are stretched beyond 300,000 kilometres. Regular maintenance is sometimes curtailed because of slim profit margins.

In the highly competitive taxi industry, taxicab drivers rarely show unity. But disunity isn't an insurmountable obstacle. In the summer of 2005, fifty taxicab drivers parked their cars to protest what the drivers thought was an "unfair" increase in stand rent.

During the George Street Festival, a six-day event in late July, an estimated 120,000 people pass through the gates. By three o'clock in the morning, the bars have emptied and the patrons spill out in search of taxicabs.

The City's Teeming Entrails

■▼■▼■▼■▼■▼■▼■▼■▼

Scenes from the Underground

"No driver shall knowingly drive persons known to him to be engaged in an unlawful act."
– St. John's Municipal Act, 1921

"I don't feel safe downtown. Time was, people would stand on the wharves and come up and say, 'How are you, boy?' and be after inviting you home and all this. Proper thing! But my dear: it's some different these past ten or twelve years. I'd not go near the place now! All those bars, and no shops, and all these people wandering round on drugs, or something. And no one saying hello. I'm scared to go there now."
– Bridie O'Brien, at the Brady House Detoxification Centre, as recounted in Neigel Rapport, *Talking Violence: An Anthropological Interpretation of Conversation in the City*

*"Well, it's like the name says, down*town.*"*
– Anonymous Royal Newfoundland Constabulary officer, from Peter McGahan, *Police Images of a City*

For some taxicab drivers, offshore oil has become the symbol of all that is wrong in our urban culture: the drugs, the violent crime and the prostitution. Black gold is ruining Newfoundland's traditional way of life. In fact, this logic has become so popular that it is largely accepted by the public and reinforced by the media, the police and social action groups. The line of reasoning goes something like this: crime follows money. Even as early as 1984, in a report prepared by the RCMP, "Impact of Offshore Oil," the author predicted that "increased affluence will create problems."

But is crime really on the rise? Because taxicab drivers who work the night shift reiterate seemingly endless stories of drug addicts and prostitutes, one might begin to think that, in fact, a drug-fuelled crime wave was sweeping through St. John's and quickly spreading out beyond the overpass. It's essential not to take these taxicab stories out of context. Taxicab drivers are regularly exposed to a side of life most people don't know exists and will probably never see. In fact, taxicab drivers are often active links and ready guides between their clients and the underground economy, earning extra cash by connecting customers with prostitutes, drugs and bootleg liquor. They first gained access to these outside earnings when nightclubs, hotels and massage parlours began to spring up in the late 1970s and early 1980s.

Statistics Canada has reported that barely 1 per cent of Canadians have used hard drugs like cocaine. In fact, the number has dropped since 2004 from 1.9 per cent to 1.2 per cent. But, in an article entitled "Fighting a Growing Problem," *The Telegram* said, "Drug use in St. John's has gotten so widespread that buying them on the street is almost as easy as buying a cup of coffee." Then-RNC Chief Joe Brown went on to state, "Every neighbourhood has someone selling drugs."

Anecdotal evidence, like the stories from taxicab drivers included in this section, appears to confirm that cocaine use, for instance, has become widespread. Because Social Services pays taxicab companies to shuttle their clients to and from methadone treatments, some taxicab drivers see a proverbial conveyor belt of misery pass through their backseat. According to one taxicab driver, "This is big business for the company." Substance abuse is nothing new, though, and rates have only increased marginally since 1997.

Statistics can be easily misread and manipulated, and social scientists have long since questioned their use as indicators of crime rates. Consider that crime reporting has increased and so has police enforcement. Since the announcement of the Hibernia discovery in 1979, the RNC, which once did the vast majority of its patrolling on foot, has grown exponentially and has become far more professional. Its area of operation has also greatly expanded. Since 1981, it has patrolled Mount Pearl and now operates in both Corner Brook and Labrador West. Thirty years ago, the Morals and Drug Section—a now extinct department of the RNC which also investigated prostitution—consisted of only five officers. The number of officers focused on such crimes is now much larger.

Drugs didn't just wash up on our shores when the offshore oil came online, and neither did prostitution. Street prostitutes worked from the harbour and the east end of Water Street servicing foreign fishing vessels long before the advent of oil. Male prostitutes once walked the strip between Hill O' Chips and the Lower Battery in the west end of downtown. The East End Club and the Esquire were known to be regularly frequented by prostitutes. Nor was prostitution the only illicit activity police once had to contend with. Bootlegging was once rampant. In Peter McGahan's study of the Royal Newfoundland Constabulary, one former constable stated, "We had anywhere from ten to twelve bootleggers in the Princess Street area alone."

Not too long ago, poverty, not affluence, bore the brunt of the blame for crime. Places like Buckmaster's Circle, Cashin Avenue and Chalker Place were thought to be where all the drugs came out of and all the stolen goods went into. But drugs don't just affect the public housing projects and the inmates at Her Majesty's Penitentiary. There is the guy heading home from a downtown binge scrunched behind the seat sniffing cocaine off a house key. There are the two drug-addled teenagers trying to sell stolen meat to feed their addiction. This is the world that taxi drivers inhabit. Their stories expose the dark underbelly of St. John's. But, as sociologist Elliot Leyton once pointed out, increasing awareness of a problem doesn't mean that the problem is increasing.

Over Aggressive—That's One Way to Put It

Darryl, driving and dispatching for forty years

According to Mothers Against Drunk Driving, in 2009, alcohol was a contributing factor in over 60,000 car crash injuries in Canada. While the rate of impaired driving has decreased over the last twenty-five years, the taxicab drivers were clear that it once plagued the industry. Of course, drinking and driving is a problem for society, not just the taxi industry. In fact, most career drivers are adamant that they have never driven a cab while intoxicated. Some, however, admitted to drinking and driving in their youth. But not all taxi drivers are drunks, just as not everyone who stumbles out of a downtown club at three in the morning will get behind the wheel of a car.

When I first started out back in the late '70s, drinking and driving was rampant. You got to look at the era. No one went downtown like they do now. Everyone went to house parties and drove home. But people drove slower and there was a lot less cars on the road because a lot less people owned cars.

Take my father, for example.

As soon as school was let out for the summer, we used to go around the bay. There'd be Mom and Dad, us youngsters, probably a few cousins, maybe an aunt or an uncle, all loaded up in the biscuit truck. There'd be beds and dressers, everything in the truck, the whole family in the wooden box in the back of the truck.

If I head out there now, it's an hour and fifteen minutes. I've done it in an hour. With Dad, it took three hours, and sometimes four or five hours. Sometimes we wouldn't get there until dark.

There's a good reason for that. I'm sure Dad bought a beer at every club on the way out, him and my uncle. He could be full to the gills and drive around the bay no sweat. It wasn't that Dad could drive better drunk; it was the way he drove. Besides, it wasn't him you had to worry about; you had to worry about the idiots who ran through the stop signs at 100 clicks an hour.

You shouldn't drink and drive—that's not the point. The point is people drove and went a certain pace. Life was slower. It wasn't that way with the taxis. Some of us were over aggressive—that's one way to put it.

Super Ace was an old-school stand. Most of the drivers down there were either retired or career taxi drivers. Back then, you couldn't buy beer in the stores, and retailers didn't open until nine o'clock. Whoever was on a job closest to nine would buy the beer and bring it back to the stand. In the run of a week, it'd be nothing to have fifty or sixty dozen beer bottles to take back to the brewery.

All hands were at it. It was a culture of boozebags.

I don't know how some of us never got killed, or worse. Joe Budgell was full one night and drove his car over an island and hauled the stop sign right up the chassis. With the car half off the ground and resting on the pole, Joe got down out of her and walked back to the stand with two or three lanes of traffic at a standstill watching the whole thing. Mel Kennedy worked with me at Capital Taxi. He bought a brand new Pontiac Parisienne, the one with the chrome splash panels high up on the door. She was gorgeous—an absolute gem. Not two weeks after he got her, right out of the wrapper, he had her parked down on Harvey Road, and another cabbie, loaded, opened her up from bumper to bumper. Poor Mel never got a cent out of it and had to get the car fixed himself. He drove that car for four years with the whole side Polybonded to shit. Every time I saw him get out of that car, I almost cried.

We used to call them "boo-boos."

When you got back to the stand, there was always the usual questions from the operator: *Is she wrote off? Was it your fault? Can we get her on the road for a shift tomorrow evening?* They never asked anything like *Are you all right? Are the passengers hurt?* No matter who you talk to, that's the way it was. Getting the car back on the road was the number one priority.

You might've heard talk of how in the 1950s the cops and the fire department were at odds with one another. Sometimes the cops would show up at a fire and they'd be in the firemen's way and they would get sprayed down. It was the same scenario with the cops and taxi drivers. Once or twice a week, you'd hear over the radio that a kid was missing. The first place the cops would phone was the taxi stands. *Everyone keep an eye out for little Jimmy wearing an orange coat. He's gone missing.* It's a numbers game. We got 364 cabs on the road, more than there were cops in the city.

But the cops had it burned up their arse about drivers flying around town. They were sick of it, and the provincial government was sick of it. That's when they introduced the points system. From their perspective, we were all guilty of something and it was just a matter of time before they figured out what.

A lot of those drivers were weekend warriors. They'd come out on a Friday with a pillow in the back so they could stay in the car and whack it to it and get a couple hundred for themselves. It'd be nothing for them to zoom down Water Street in the middle of the night doing 100 kilometres an hour trying to make the money as fast as they could. With hundreds of people stood up down around the stand, some of them out in the middle of the road trying to flag down cabs, there was bound to be accidents. One buddy popped a missus up over the bonnet and in through the windshield, like a moose. I think she died.

I had a customer in the car, a driver we all avoided like the plague. He was a real bastard when he was drinking. One Friday night, no one would pick him up, and I volunteered. It was a decent length of a run, and I wanted him out of the car as soon as possible. Flying up LeMarchant Road, the arse of her wasn't even through the lights at Prince of Wales Street, which had just turned red, when the cop's lights flashed. Cab drivers use a lot of foresight when it comes to traffic lights. Most people wouldn't because they don't drive enough to take heed. And not all traffic lights are the same. But if you're driving a cab long enough and passing them every day you know just how long they take to change. I could time some of them down to the second, I'm sure.

So I pulled in.

"You're in an awful rush tonight," the cop said.

"Yeah, I am," I said. "Look who I got in the back."

He was a hard case; the cops knew he was a hard case. He had a record as long as your sleeve: possession, assault, theft. "I pity you, but I have to give you a ticket," the cop explained. "If you were going a bit slower, I could've let you away with it."

Getting the drunks off the street wasn't much of an excuse anymore.

Having said that, the drug of choice now is crack, cocaine, or pills. It's a bad set up. The last time I taxied was 1995, I think. That stand was pretty clean. It wasn't yet bleeding into the place. But it's a bad setup now. Don't get me wrong. There were guys drinking and driving and smoking dope, no doubt, but there were probably only a few who were into the hard stuff, and it was nowhere near the level it's at today. I'm not targeting them, because they were no different than any other stand. If you went to just about any stand and asked them what level of drug use is on the go they would tell you that no one there smokes dope. They're all basically full of shit. Any stand you want to mention is the same.

Dispatching one night, this guy, Craig, was driving his shift on acid. The stand owner realized he definitely wasn't high on something like a draw of weed, because you can tell the difference. Anyone who has had any involvement with drugs on any level knows if someone is on more than weed. You can tell, right? Craig, he's whacked on acid and driving a taxi. The stand owner used to spend a bit of time downtown. It would be nothing for him to come out of the club and to check out the stand and see what's on the go. He took the car and fired him. The next night, he gave him another car and another shift.

I thought about this one today. It was a bad accident, but it was a stupid accident. Chris Clark was a lunatic. He found out his wife was fucking around on him and drove his car right into some club downtown, right on in through the club. When he taxied in the early '80s, he used to drive a little Ford Fairmont. He was drag racing and missed the turn by Portugal Cove Road and New Cove Road and went right up onto the pole. It was totally reckless, and he got fired. This happened after I got off, sometime after the twelve o'clock shift ended. I didn't know it had happened until I went to work the next day. That afternoon, he phoned one of the brokers who had cars down to the stand. He put Chris in one. The stand owner fired him, and one of the brokers hired him again that same afternoon. There are worse things that have happened.

The broker said, "Take the car, and lay low. But don't go near the stand."

What does Chris do? As soon as he got the car, he came down over the hill. At the time, you used to have to go to our standby stand a few streets over. You had to go park there and wait to be called to go over, because we were only allowed four cars there at any one time. You'd rotate, basically. Meanwhile, I had heard that he'd had an accident the night before, but I didn't know the details. I called a few more cars to come over, and one of them happened to be Chris's.

"Next at the standby."

"Seven."

"All right," I said. "Come over."

Sure enough, he pulled up. He got out of his car, and the stand owner looked out the window. As calm as anything, he said, "Come up, I want you for a second, Chris."

I might be a bit dramatic, but this is the way I remember how it went down. There was a big set of steps on the back of the dispatch office, and I could hear Chris coming up. As soon as I heard his feet hit the floor, I heard a pop. The stand owner dropped him like a sack of potatoes. Blood and snots went everywhere. After all was said and done, Chris got himself together and went back out and worked his shift. If it was my car, I would've given me a good punch in the face, too. It was because of what he had done to the car. It's one thing to be in an accident speeding on a straightaway and hitting a gravel patch. If you're drag racing and you put a car up on the pole, man, that's over the top.

Do you know what the ongoing joke at the stand was for a long, long time? *You got no taxi licence, because you haven't been fired yet.* If you got fired today, don't worry about it, you can have a car at four o'clock the next day for your shift that night. Don't sweat it.

I Won't Touch a Drop

Theodore, driving for thirty-eight years

I remember two years in a row on New Year's Eve I got a $100 tip for taking guys home and not bringing them to their parked car. I wouldn't take them to their car. No, sir. I've often been going down Water Street and Duckworth Street and saw someone who was going to their car drunk. I'd pull over and say, "If you get in that car, I'll phone the police." This is a 24/7 city. You can't be out there driving around drunk. I'm sixty years old, and I've done my share of it. Jesus, when I was around twenty or twenty-one all of us were drinking and driving. But the traffic wasn't on the roads. At one time, you could drive from Torbay Road to the Goulds and you might run into two or three cars.

But I got nailed in 1980, and that taught me a lesson.

The last time I drove someone around looking for their car, I think the meter went up to $50. The man was gone—he was gone. He said, "Help me find my car."

I said, "Where is it to?"

"I don't know."

"Now you're in some cruel old shape. Where do you usually park?"

This was when they first opened the parking garage down by City Hall. They used to use the one up in Sebastian Court. I tried there. Nothing. I went up and down Duckworth Street. I went down Water Street. I went up and down all the side streets. You know where we found the car? On the wrong side of the road up over Amherst Street.

There ended up being fifty-odd dollars on the meter. Back then that was real coin.

This is what buddy said to me: "I couldn't get a taxi."

I told him, "Next time, leave the car home. As long as you haven't got the car, the temptation isn't there." Phone the stand until you get through, or book the cab in advance. But don't take your car downtown.

I hate to think that there are guys out there drinking and driving a taxi. I just can't see it. There's a time and place for everything.

No one likes a bottle of beer more than I do. But I won't touch a drop while I'm in this car.

The Rich Man's Drug

Frank, driving for twenty-nine years

A taxicab driver rushed into a convenience store to get gas and to grab a snack before he hit the road again. Behind him, a young man hauled up in a new truck and asked the clerk if he was interested in buying some fresh meat: steaks, chicken, fish. To the taxicab driver, the stuff was clearly hot. When the young man left, there was talk at the counter that he was somehow involved in drugs. On the floors and on the back seats of taxis, drivers often find discarded baggies with knots tied at the top. It's from customers having a "bump," or a quick fix. Throughout the city, taxis drop off strung out twenty-somethings to all-night parties, to crack houses, where they go to get high. Because taxicab drivers service every segment of our society—the lower class, the middle class, the upper class, the rich and the poor—the interviews included in the following monologues offer a glimpse into the pervasiveness of drug use.

Cocaine used to be called the "rich man's drug." Most people who used to be doing coke were doctors, lawyers and judges. But I'm not going to get into that very much. People my age beating around couldn't afford coke. You weren't working, and if you were working you were only making three or four bucks an hour. At that time, I think minimum wage was $2.85. You couldn't afford $100 for a gram of cocaine. But now it seems that since the oil came on stream, since they started paying people forty or fifty bucks an hour to make beds in Bull Arm, the drug of choice, even with the kids, is cocaine.

I was down to a house two or three nights ago, and a young guy and his buddy got in the car. "Where are you going?" I asked.

"Livingstone Street."

I knew what they were going for. They were going for coke. That's how you find out about an awful lot of things. They thought they were being right secretive. Little did they know, I dropped off twenty-five people there last week.

You're hard-pressed to go around this city and find a draw of weed or a draw of hash. But if you took a handful of nickels to George Street tomorrow night and fired them into a crowd at least half a dozen of them nickels would hit off someone selling cocaine. It could be your next-door neighbour, and you wouldn't know. I'm after bringing them up to Road De Luxe, to a $500,000 house, and they're knocking on buddy's door at four o'clock and five o'clock in the morning looking for coke.

Let me tell you something, old buddy. I can get every drug in this city that you want, right now. I can leave here and in twenty minutes we'll probably have a big chunk of hash, we'll have an ounce of weed, or a kilo of coke. That doesn't sit well with me. It's the ruination of a lot of good men and a lot of good women. You go down to the jail right now and do a survey of 100 inmates. Ninety-five per cent of them are in there for drug and alcohol-related problems. Drank too much and got on the pills and got on the coke. You can be sure, drugs and alcohol will be a factor in 95 per cent of your research. There's where your problem is to. The problem isn't the joint buddy smoked on the corner last night and got stoned.

You'll find a lot of your cokeheads at the strip clubs. For whatever reason, strip clubs and cocaine go hand-in-hand. You can't find one without finding the other. If you were an undercover cop and you were looking for cocaine, all you got to do is drive a taxi, or visit a strip joint. You'll get all the information you want. That's been my experience. I don't care what strip club it is—I don't give a monkey's Jesus—if there are girls stripping, they're doing cocaine in that club. The strippers are doing the cocaine, the patrons are doing the cocaine, and the bar staff is doing the cocaine. I don't like to tar everyone with the same brush, but it's in every single establishment.

This job here, a lot of drivers are doing cocaine, and they're doing pills. For the life of me, I can't believe that there's not a drug testing policy in place. Your daughter gets her license and parks her car Friday night and gets a taxi downtown. She does the right thing. On her way home, she gets one of the cokeheads that are driving. He's wired and has an accident and kills your daughter. Your daughter is dead because of some asshole that was driving her home. There has to be a drug testing policy put in place for anybody driving the public. If you're driving a bus or a taxi and you're driving other people's youngsters you should have to be tested for drugs. In order for you to get that Class 4 driver's licence you should have to do a drug test every few months.

It's more rampant than anybody wants to admit. For whatever reason, the night shift seems to be more affected. Ten or fifteen per cent of what's on nights are drug users. I guess it's a factor of a lot of things. You're not checked, for one. It's the only job I know of where you can come to work stoned and go home stoned and nobody ever gives a shit. If you walked into an office tomorrow and you were stoned, your boss, or your supervisor, would say, "Listen, I believe you got a problem. You appear to be stoned." You can get found out. With this job here, nobody gives a fuck. But, eventually, that is going to cause somebody's death. It's amazing that it hasn't already.

I know a school bus driver, and he has a plastic cigarette pack your father or mother might have used for rolled cigarettes. He's got one full of dope, full of joints. He got thirty or forty of them done up in cigarettes. He'll smoke some of them before his shift that night. The same guy drives a school bus, drives small kids in the daytime. How would you like that, sending your kid out to school tomorrow morning knowing the bus driver is whacked right out of his mind?

An Eye-Opening Experience
Bazil, driving and dispatching for twelve years
Coming into the taxi industry was definitely an eye-opening experience. People who are Monday-to-Friday, regular office-types, have no idea what the world is all about. Think about St. John's. We

have all the amenities of a big city, but we have a small community. Everything is more hidden, that's all. You can get anything you want in St. John's. I know how to find most of it, and I don't even fuck around. I even know hookers by their first name. I see Chrissie out there, and I'm after pulling in on a cold night and letting her sit in the car for ten or fifteen minutes. I'll give her a cigarette and let her warm up. What are you going to do? It's not that busy. So what if she's a hooker? She still got to make a living.

My brother died of Lou Gehrig's disease. There were times towards the end of his life when he was in extreme pain. The only way he could get rid of the pain was to roll up some cocaine and a bit of weed and smoke a nice little joint. He would call me on Friday night, and I'd go and pick it up for him. I would never know where to find that stuff if I wasn't taxiing.

A Dealer on Every Corner
Theodore, driving for thirty-eight years

The first time I ever saw cocaine was years before it was big here. That was 1987, or maybe 1988. I picked a guy up at the Village Mall. He was full of tattoos and hung out at the pinball place that used to be there. He got in, and I drove him to Foxtrap. He said, "Do you want cash, or do you want this." He opened up a tube of aluminum foil and there was white powder sprinkled all through it. "That's $1,000 worth of coke."

"No, thanks," I said. "I got enough problems without adding to them."

I was away from the taxiing for about eight years, and I went to the mainland. When I came home, I couldn't believe how much cocaine was in this town. There's pretty much a dealer on every corner. Like that one that got busted down on Casey Street. There's another one across from that, a little further west, and another one up over a store across the way. It's everywhere. I don't know why people do it. I've seen people lose their homes, their wives and their kids and good salaries all over this stupid white powder that does nothing but kill them.

I had a guy get in the back. He picked up his buddy down by George Street, and they went around the corner to a rub-and-tug. He said, "I got something for a bit of leverage with the girls." He knocked on the door, but they'd already gone to bed.

He got out, and his buddy had me take him to Empire Avenue. On the way back, he scrunched down behind the seat, and I could hear the sniff, sniff. What he was doing was putting the cocaine in the groove of the house key and snorting it before he got home so his wife wouldn't know what he was up to.

Reapers

Danny, driving for three years

I picked up a young couple on Cabot Street. The girl sat in the front, and the guy sat in the back. It was after four-thirty in the morning. I asked buddy, "Where are we going?"

"Up to Sobeys on Merrymeeting Road." I made a right on Lemarchant Road, and he said, "No need to be nervous, man."

I looked at him in the rear-view mirror: "What do you mean, 'No need to be nervous'? Now I am nervous."

His girlfriend was like, "No, no—we're fine."

But he kept saying, "No, man. Chill out, man."

I stopped the car and said, "You guys got to get out. No offence, but that's enough."

The two of them were crackheads. I call them "reapers." After four-thirty in the morning, you run into a lot of reapers. You run into the crowd that are drug addicted—the crackheads. You know what the grim reaper looks like? Reapers look like that. They wear hoodies, and they're skinned right out. There's no weight on their bodies. That was one of my first experiences with them. I was like, *Hold on now. Is this going to happen every time I pick someone up at this hour in the morning?* I found that after four-thirty up until about six o'clock you run into a lot of reapers. They go to crack house parties. They're running drugs, and they're running booze.

Reapers are the most dangerous people in the city. They'll feel you out right away; they'll make eye contact with you. At first, they'll usually say something stupid: "I'm just going to my buddy's house to get a few sniffs, a few snorts." And then they usually ask, "Where are you from, buddy?" They're feeling you out. And they're looking at you, too. They're looking at your sweater, your clothes, your chains and your watch. Then they're looking up in your visor because they know cab drivers put cash up there.

We have day shift drivers who handle them differently. They're stern. They don't tolerate any bullshit. They want the money up front. One time, I asked a guy if he had the money, and there was a bit of an altercation. Since then, I try not to ask.

Here in Newfoundland the reapers kind of shocked me. I was in Toronto for five years, and I knew there was a subculture of drug addicts and crackheads. But I didn't think it was as serious as it is here. Reapers are pretty creepy and sneaky people. You won't see them out in the daytime—no way. They're vampirish. They're reapers.

Stolen Meat

Bazil, driving and dispatching for twelve years

Two guys from down around Pasadena Crescent were going around talking about selling some meat they had stolen from Sobeys. They asked if they could pay me with it. "No thanks. I don't buy anything hot," I said. "Besides, even if I did, how do I know you never found that in the dumpster? That could've been there all day."

"Oh, no—that's fresh."

"I don't take goods. I only take cash," I said.

I brought them to a house up on New Pennywell Road. I can't remember the number. But they went in and sold the meat, came back and had me take them down to Shopper's Drug Mart on Empire Avenue. He was going to get his methadone. On the way, he called his drug dealer to bring him his weed. They got beer somewhere, too, and paid me out of the money they got for the meat.

On the Rob

Sandra, driving for four years

There are nights when I get completely wigged out, like incidents that I can't shake off. You might get a pillhead, for instance, or you might get somebody who is on the rob. If you get some dude who you think might be up to no good, you know you could get accidently wrapped up in it, you might get unintentionally involved. Two or three days later, I'm like the post-traumatic stress case. You start to wonder about every customer. You start to question your own judgement. I'm wondering why I don't want to go to work. I'm wondering why I want to go home and call it quits.

I picked up this young guy on Kelsey Drive, and he had a cart at a store that didn't have carts. I knew right away something sketchy was going on. He told me he'd load up the trunk himself. Typically, to be polite, you would do it, or at least help him do it. When he was loading up, I could feel the weight of what he was putting in the trunk push down the coiled wire springs. I knew I had a load of hot gear in the back of the car. When he got in, he was all out of breath, and he told me where we were going. I knew when he gave me the address where I was going. I knew how bad that could end up. Within a three week period, people there have been arrested with weapons, and this same guy had been in a chase with the cops.

As we were going down Kenmount Road, he said, "Do you mind if I take my medicine?"

He hauled out a pill bottle and a metal car charger, crushed up a pill on a credit card and snorted it back without even trying not to be seen, without even trying to hide down behind the seat.

I Got to Move My Stuff

Frank, driving for twenty-nine years

I had a call to go up to Barachois Street behind the Village Mall. It was about two o'clock in the morning. I went there and tooted the horn, and this guy came out. "Put the meter on, man," he said. "Myself and the old lady had a big fight, and she's gone to her mother's place. She told me to get out, so I got to move all my stuff out. I got it all packed up by the door ready to go."

He started lugging up a few things, a VCR, a TV, a dresser.

"Let me give you a hand," I said. "It won't cost you as much."

I went down and he filled up the car and I brought him down to Forbes Street. He paid me, and I went on my way.

The next day I get a call from the dispatcher: "You got to call constable so-and-so down at the RNC." Lo and behold, buddy was robbing that apartment where I picked him up, and I was helping him. But I had no idea. I told the cop where I dropped him off and everything was hunky dory. The cop believed me. He said he would call me back if he needed anything else. But he never did.

A Backyard Tour of Duckworth Street

Gordon, driving for eighteen years

A buddy of mine was driving past Kentucky Fried Chicken on Duckworth Street when a guy came running out with a ski mask on. He had a butcher knife in one hand and a bag of money in the other. Paddy's not really a fighter, but he has a good sense of what's right and what's wrong. When the guy came out of the store, Paddy chased after him. Buddy took him on a backyard tour around Duckworth Street. He climbed up over a bunch of fences, and Paddy ripped him down and sat on him until the police came. The next day in the paper: "Police apprehended a man." There was no mention of Paddy chasing him down all over hell's half-acre and risking his life.

The police always make themselves look good, but they'll come around looking for help. I remember they came around looking for a brand new Caprice which was stolen right off the RNC parking lot. I saw the guy driving around because it was a lousy paint job, and the big silver Constabulary crest was showing right through the paint. And they couldn't find that car? Buddy was driving it around like it was his own, day and night. I ran into him a dozen times.

They came up to the stand looking for it. "Anyone see that?"

"I saw the guy driving around," I said. "It's a bad paint job, though. The crest is showing right through the paint. I'm after running into him a dozen times."

They found it in the ghetto down on Little Street up on blocks. Everything was gone out of it; she was stripped down to the bone.

Who Flushed All the Ecstasy Down the Toilet?

Walter, driving for twenty-three years

This guy I drove somewhere once, a drunk, phoned back and said, "I left my medication in the car." The driver picked it up, and it was Oxycontin. He just flushed it down the toilet. I would do the same thing.

I picked up this young girl. She might've been sixteen, and she was out of her mind. When she got up and left the car, I looked back and there was this tiny little pointer light. I picked it up, but it didn't work. I flicked the switch and figured the batteries were dead. I opened it up, and here it was full of ecstasy. I went in and flushed the stuff down the toilet. One of the guys—he ended up punching the dispatcher in the face one night and got thrown out of the stand—was in the bathroom and said, "Who flushed all the ecstasy down the toilet?"

"Me," I said.

"What did you do that for? I could've sold that for loot."

"I'm not adding to someone else's misery," I said. "It's my ecstasy, and I'll do whatever the fuck I want with it."

The Government Pays a Fortune

Bazil, driving and dispatching for twelve years

We drive a lot of the methadone people. The government pays a fortune to get them back and forth to the drugstores. This is big business for some of the stands.

Some of these people are eighteen years old and you got to bring them down to line up to get their methadone. I guess it's a testament to the amount of drugs that's on the go when you see all of these young people on this program. You go to a drugstore that's dispensing the methadone and all you see are taxis dropping them off to go in and get their methadone. It's sad.

It doesn't seem like many people get off the program, either. I thought that with methadone they weaned you down off of it. They decrease your dose to try to get you off of it. At least, that's the way they do it up in British Columbia. There's one guy I've been driving for four years, and his dose hasn't come down at all. He's been taking the same dose for the last four years. They're just giving them this drug so they're not craving Oxycontin and out committing armed robberies to pay for it.

What Happens Between You and the Driver

Frank, driving for twenty-nine years

You can go to your doctor and say, "I've been smoking pot all my life, and I can't get off it." They'll put you on methadone. It's as simple as that. Poof—you're on it! "I got a cocaine habit." Poof—you're on it! You got a lot of people out there who wake up in the morning and say, "Where am I going to get my next buzz to?" That means they're too far gone into their coke, or they're too far gone into their Oxycontin. Methadone is a version of heroin—that's all. It takes away the edge. They're giving the addicts the buzz for nothing.

For instance, take buddy on Queen's Road. He'll call us at ten to eight every morning. He goes up to Shoppers Drug Mart, and he's the first one in line. If he can't make it, he'll call. The boys even know his authorization number, it's gotten that bad. Everybody gets an authorization number. If you're on welfare and you have a doctor's appointment, you call your social worker, and then they'll call us to approve a taxi. The Department of Social Services will authorize us to pick you up at your house, bring you to your doctor and, when you're ready, drop you back home again. Then we'll bill Social Services based on the information provided.

There's a good example, a crackhead who wants to sell his charge slip. [*He points out the window to a young couple sitting on the sidewalk.*] He's got an $80 slip to go up to Paradise Medical Clinic. This guy gets his methadone at Downtown Pharmacy, but every week he gets authorization to go to Paradise Medical Clinic. He'll turn around and sell that $80 charge to a driver for thirty bucks to buy dope. But what happens between you and the driver happens between you and the driver. When a driver normally comes home with fifty bucks, and now he got a chance to come home with seventy or eighty bucks, I'm not going to say anything.

There Are No Prostitutes in St. John's

Theodore, driving for thirty-eight years

Melissa Ditmore, chair of the New York-based Sex Workers' Project, has pointed out that 85 per cent of New York sex workers operate indoors. In a study which focused on fifty sex trade workers, Behind Closed Doors: An Analysis of Indoor Sex Workers in New York City, *she determined that while only 15 per cent of prostitutes work the streets, they account for an overwhelming number of arrests. Her findings share many similarities with other North American cities, including St. John's, where prostitutes work in places like brothels, massage parlors, private homes and bars. Often it is only when communities complain about sex workers lingering in their neighbourhoods and police focus on sweeps and arrests that the public are made aware of them. The corner of Church Hill and Duckworth Street has long been*

*known to be frequented by street prostitutes. CBC reported that over
a two-month span six prostitutes and nine Johns were arrested in the
area. Reinforced with images of discarded condoms, the reporter
stated, "Everyone knows they're working the street to feed their drug
addiction." But most sex workers enter the profession in times of financial vulnerability, and only a minority get involved because of drug
abuse.*

*The indoor sex trade has not been widely investigated. In fact,
most studies focus on street prostitution. Because the sex trade industry is largely invisible, existing behind closed doors, the perception remains popular that there are no prostitutes in St. John's. But the
common themes in the following monologues suggest that data col-
lected by the Sex Workers Project reflect systematic phenomena and
is not merely anecdotal.*

I picked up this young girl working security on the east end of
downtown. "What are you doing down here tonight?" I asked her.

"Why? What's wrong with this end of town?" she said.

"This is where the hookers come to get picked up."

"What are you talking about?" she said. "There are no prostitutes in St. John's."

"There are no prostitutes in St. John's? I'll show you something
on the way there now, just to prove my point."

I went up Duckworth Street right to the corner of Church Hill
and Duckworth Street and there was this young one stood up. She
was about seventeen years old. "Do you see her right there? If I stop
this car she's getting aboard, and we're going off and having sex.
That's what she's waiting there for." I went to the corner of Gower
Street and Church Hill and there was another one. "See that one?
She's pimping herself out for a few bucks."

"You're not serious?" she said.

"That's why I asked you what you were doing in this end of
town."

"I'm not going down there no more," she said.

A Common Practice
Bazil, driving and dispatching for twelve years

If you come in from out of town and you're looking for companionship for the night, a cab driver usually knows somebody. The girl might say, "If you know anyone looking for a date, here's my number." That's a common practice between prostitutes and cab drivers. They'll use a certain taxi on a consistent basis to solicit their business for them.

Keep It in Your Pants
Mark, driving for twenty-one years

I used to drive around a prostitute, Tatiana. When she went out on a call, she never used any other taxi driver but me, unless I wasn't on the road. One night in particular, we started six or seven o'clock and by eight-thirty the next morning her phone was still going. I did my bit and slept in the car with the seat back waiting by the phone. Every time she would come out from doing a John she'd throw the money in my lap: "Hold onto that for me." I mean, I had a couple thousand dollars in front of me. She got out of the car that morning and gave me three or four hundred bucks. That's a nice big pay. If she needed a loan of money during the week, or if she needed a dozen beer or a pack of smokes, I had no problem giving it to her. I knew I'd get it back, plus some.

Tatiana wasn't her real name. As a matter of fact, I don't even know her real name.

One time, she offered me money to do her. I said, "No. I'll do you when you win a million." That was our little joke.

She used to say, "One of these days, I'm going to win that million, and you're doing me."

It's like anything else, I suppose. You want what you can't have.

The short and long of it is you got to be honest. This is not a racket to be at if you're going to keep secrets from your wife. The phone can't ring at one or two o'clock at night and you got to hide around the corner with the phone. If you can't keep your dick in your pants this is not a job to be at. Your marriage will suffer, trust me on that. If you're married, you can't have girlfriends or flings while you're taxiing. Somebody will see you with her, and that somebody will phone your wife. I was at home one night, and the phone rang. My wife answered. "Do you know where your husband is to tonight? He's out fucking around on you." Missus went on and on and on and on.

Eventually, my wife said, "Listen, honey, I don't know who you're supposed to be talking to, but you're obviously talking to the wrong person. My husband is sat right here along side of me. Would you like to talk to him?"

My wife's friends had a problem with it more than my wife did: "I can't believe you're letting him drive these women around."

"What do you mean, 'I'm letting him drive these women around?'" she said. "That's his fucking job. What's he going to do? I don't let him do nothing. He still got to pay the bills at the end of the month."

What Happened to the Business?

Ronald, driving for twenty-five years

Some social scientists say it is environmental influences—where the taxicab drivers were brought up, their "cultural determinism"—which has kept some tied to the underclass. Others point to economic systems and their institutions, in this case, the stand owners and the municipal regulators, a theory known as "structuralism." Most, however, like famed sociologist Denis Gilbert, would agree that the culture of taxicab drivers, which includes bootlegging, is a "response to social constraints and opportunities of the structural conditions that generated it."

It was a good stand with twenty-seven cars and lots of work. And then they started bootlegging. It got so bad that the dispatcher used to have bottles of rum down at the office in the east end. If you phoned for a taxi, they used to say, "That'll be twenty minutes, or half an hour." But if you phoned for a bottle of rum, you'd have it right away.

It all boils down to caring. The dispatcher didn't care about the customer getting a taxi. He wasn't making anything off that. But the guy who wanted a bottle of rum would get that bottle of rum right away because the dispatcher was pocketing $20. You'd get your rum right away, but you wouldn't get your taxi right away.

What happened to the business? It slowly disintegrated to nothing. Customer service was always good until the dispatcher realized he could make money selling booze. The owner didn't care. He was half-cracked. They never had a psychiatric assessment done on him, but he wasn't all there. If there were fifteen complaints against the stand in one night, he owned eleven of them.

The Constabulary knew it was going on. Yes, Jesus, I'd say the cops bought booze off them. It's like anything else. The cops know everything. They know who is selling drugs, to who and where and how and when. But do you bother with it? Do you gather up a task force to do it? I don't think so.

Hacked to Death

Work-Related Violence

"If someone comes up to my cab and I don't like their looks, I'm not going to take them. I don't care if the police tell me, and I go to jail. I'd rather get a hacking violation than wind up in the city hospital."
– Boston taxi driver, *PBS: Forum 38*

"Each night when I return the cab to the garage, I have to clean the cum off the back seat. Some nights, I clean off the blood."
– Travis Bickle (Robert de Niro), *Taxi Driver*

Each week, thousands of people frequent George Street and the dozens of bars and restaurants in the downtown core. In fact, the George Street Association boasts it has more bars per square-foot than anywhere else in North America. On any given Friday or Saturday night, thousands of people could be on the street. During the George Street Festival, a six-day event in late July, an estimated 120,000 people pass through the gates. By three o'clock in the morning, the bars have emptied and the drunken patrons spill out in search of taxicabs. Many linger around until the early hours of the morning. Assaults and vandalism are not uncommon. In recent years, the Royal Newfoundland Constabulary has increased their presence by putting more boots on the ground and stationing patrol cars at the main entrance. Closed-circuit cameras have also been installed. George Street is big business for both the city and the province. They're simply protecting their investment.

When other forms of public transportation are reduced, the taxi industry becomes an integral part of the nighttime economy.

Unlike downtown business owners who are afforded a number of safeguards, little has been done at either the civic or provincial levels to help ensure a safe working environment for taxicab drivers. Yet, according to a 2010 report by Statistics Canada, taxiing is among the most dangerous occupations in Canada. Taxi drivers and police have the highest on-the-job risk of murder.

The Newfoundland and Labrador Occupational Health and Safety Act requires that employers "ensure the health, safety and welfare of his or her workers." Whereas in Nova Scotia the taxi licence holder is responsible for the safety of the driver, in the Newfoundland and Labrador legislation there is very little mention of taxi safety. Although the legislation requires that an employer with ten or more employees establish and maintain an occupational health and safety program, fleet owners and brokers provide little or no safety training. Within recent years, taxi companies have designated secure drop-off locations, namely gas stations, where drivers deposit cash. But safety measures are often arbitrarily implemented by the taxicab drivers themselves.

There are important lessons to be learned from other jurisdictions. Until 1986, Winnipeg was seen as a safe and friendly working environment for taxi drivers. But the fatal beating of taxi driver Gurnam Singh Dhaliwal prompted the provincial government to create a task force aimed at improving driver safety. In fact, many cities in North America and the United Kingdom now require taxicabs to be equipped with partitions. In New York, partitions are left down during the day and raised during the night. Winnipeg's response to the task force's findings, including mandatory use of cameras, partitions and the introduction of a crime-reduction program, has created arguably the safest working environment for taxicab drivers in North America. They found that protective shields were "essentially valid."

The St. John's taxicab industry has frowned on the idea of implementing partitions because it is felt they will intrude on the relationship between the driver and the customer. There is also the question of cost. Manufacturers are now keenly aware of the financial obstacles to small operators. Protective partitions are no longer modified police shields but specific to the needs of the taxi industry. Self-install shield kits are available at low cost and can be mounted in twenty minutes.

Other practical initiatives have been successful at bringing some sense of security to the occupation. Taxi marshals, municipally regulated uniformed authorities or taxi company officers, add an element of policing at stands. Closed-circuit cameras have aided in apprehending perpetrators. In Winnipeg, since the introduction of closed-circuit cameras, arrest rates for perpetrators of assaults against taxicab drivers rose by 30 per cent. In Nova Scotia, the Department of Environment and Labour has initiated a practical violence-prevention plan.

Frustrated by Newfoundland and Labrador's lack of safety measures, one young St. John's taxicab driver, the victim of a weapons-related assault, went before news cameras in March 2011. "There's no barricade, and we don't have eyes in the back of our head. It's going to take something serious to happen before anything gets done."

A Hard Case

Frank, driving for twenty-nine years

Although St. John's remains one of the safest cities in Canada, taxi drivers are frequently both the witnesses to and the victims of violent crime. A number of factors put them at risk, including carrying cash and working alone late at night in high-crime areas. Jacob Leibovitch, executive director of the iTaxiworkers' Association, an Ontario-based organization, said, "Economic pressures force cab drivers into dangerous situations." One of the key factors is that the income for drivers is so low that in many cases they're taking additional risks on the road to make the money they need to feed their families. The pattern of assault is disquietingly familiar: some presumed minor insult results in an often severe beating by a group of heavily intoxicated males; a drug-

addicted twenty-something hauls out a knife or a needle and demands cash; called to an address to pick up a fare, a taxi driver is assaulted with a weapon and robbed by two men in dark clothes; a juvenile female is charged with assault and property damage after a dispute over the fare.

For the most part, customers are pretty good. Ninety-five per cent of them that get in my car respect me, respect my job, respect my cab. But then there are about 5 per cent that think the world owes them something and that they're doing you a favour for getting in your cab and you're supposed to put up with their antics and their bullshit. That's not necessarily the way it goes. Me, personally, if you get in my car and you show me respect you'll only get respect back. But if you show me contempt, it won't be very long before you're back out on the street. Let the doorknob hit you where the good lord split you. Over the last twenty-eight years, having that type of attitude is how I've survived in this industry. I know of a lot of guys who have been punched out and robbed. You know—different things. Thankfully, I've avoided most of that.

I have to say, in the last eight or ten years, the younger crowd are much harder to deal with. It's the drugs. When we were knocking around, the drug of choice was a bit of marijuana. Now, it's Oxycontin, it's cocaine, it's ecstasy. You got Red Bull out there that'll set them out of their minds. A couple pills, a bit of Red Bull, and they don't know what they're at. If you're going to get into trouble, they're the ones you're going to get the trouble from. Them and the university students.

When the university students first come to St. John's, there are always incidents with cab drivers. No doubt. That's the first weekend back. They don't want to pay, or they get on with their macho tough guy attitude because they come from some little outport and they've been into a fight or two in their life and all of a sudden they come to St. John's to take over. Ask any cab driver who gives them the most trouble, and they'll tell you: university students. I don't even bother to pick them up.

If I can help it, I'll pick up a guy and a girl. If I'm driving downtown at three o'clock in the morning, just as the clubs are letting out, there are maybe hundreds of people walking up the streets looking for taxis. If there's a guy and a girl, I'm picking them up. I'll drive right through the centre of downtown, and I'll wait until I see a guy and a girl, or two girls, or something like that. I like to get a guy and a girl for one simple reason. He got one thing on his mind: he wants to get her home and get her drawers off. That's all he's interested in. He's not interested in causing me trouble.

You always got to be on your toes. It's not always about getting the face beat off you, either. Drivers leave here and go to Carbonear, and when they get there buddy in the back seat jumps out—he's gone. That driver is out $200, his time, his money and his gas, and he still never got paid. You're also talking about the money he didn't make on another job. If you're going to Carbonear, that's an hour and a half out and an hour and a half back. He's burned three hours' worth of gas, and he hasn't got nothing to show for it.

The first fare I ever lost was for $3.50. I went back to his girlfriend's house, knocked on the door and said, "Tell that dummy, if he's going to take off on a cab driver not to be coming out of a residential address where I can go back and find out exactly who he is."

It's becoming more frequent. In the past three or four years, I'd say I've lost eight or ten fares. About a month or two months ago, I got a call to pick someone up on Heffernan's Line in the Goulds. I pulled up in front the house, and a young woman came out. "Where you going, my love?" I asked her.

"Tim Horton's on Thorburn Road," she said.

"That's a fine old haul for a coffee."

"I'm meeting someone."

When we got there, twenty-nine bucks was on the meter. She looked in Tim Horton's, but it was empty. "He's not here yet," she said.

"Who's not there yet?" I asked.

"The guy I'm supposed to meet. He's paying for the taxi."

As soon as she said that the red flags went up. I knew something was on the go. I waited and waited and waited. Finally, I said, "I can't wait here all day, my love. You're going to have to pay me and get the money off of him."

"Oh," she said. "I left my money on the counter at home."

"Have you got a credit card?"

She had every card under the sun, but she didn't have a credit card. "It doesn't look like he's going to show," I said. "Do you know this person?"

"I don't know him. I just met him on the Internet."

Mary, Mother of Jesus. I knew then that I was in trouble.

"If you bring me back home, I'll give you the $58."

I said, "Missus, I got to ask you a question. Do I look like a total idiot to you? Do me a favour and get the hell out of my car. You haven't got the money here, and you haven't got the money home. Get out!"

I heaved her out, phoned the police and waited an hour for them to show up. The police do their calls in priority, and a taxi driver is not high on their priority list. I've sat in parking lots on a Friday night at two o'clock, waiting. You wait an hour, and then you spend the better part of another hour giving your statement. That's your Friday night gone, your gravy—two to four in the morning.

Later that night, Co-Op Taxi phoned our stand and asked the dispatcher, "Did one of your drivers pick up somebody on Heffernan's Line?"

"Yes," he said, "She owes him twenty-nine bucks."

"That's queer," he said, "because one of our cars took her home. She went into the house, and she never came out. She owes him twenty-nine bucks now, too."

There you go. That's what you're dealing with.

If someone is getting shot or stabbed, the guy getting shot or stabbed deserves more priority than me who is only out a bit of money. But when the police do show up, they're real good: "Pay the man, or you're coming with us. I'm not here for a debate. Pay the man right now, or you're coming with us." If you charge the person who refuses to pay, which you will, two or three months later, you'll get a check in the mail for what they owe you.

But a lot of people understand you're not going to pursue the matter, and they'll take full advantage of that.

In my eyes, in my car, everyone is treated equally. If you treat me with respect, you will get respect. If you treat me with contempt, you will get contempt, for about the five seconds it takes for me to stop the car: "Get out!" I'm a firm believer that life is too short to put up with any bullshit. If I didn't cause the problem, I don't want to be part of the problem.

I can talk with my mouth, or I can talk with my fists. I prefer to talk with my mouth, but if I got to, I'll talk with my fists. When university students get aboard, because of my size and the tone of my voice, they say, "You're a hard case, aren't you?"

I don't take any bullshit. If that means I'm a hard case, then I'm a hard case. Because if you come across as a wimp you might not get paid and you might get robbed.

With my two kids, they know that if I got to get out some night and knock someone's head off, I got to get out and knock someone's head off. If I come home with blood on me, they know some asshole didn't want to get out of the car, or some asshole didn't want to pay me. But they also know that if I got blood on me, the other guy got a lot more on him.

When I first started driving a cab, I didn't care much for anything that walked, creeped or crawled. If I had a problem, the only way I knew how to solve it was to put up my fists. Whoever won, the problem got solved. It was that simple. If it was still that way today this world would be a lot better place to live in. There's too many people going around now who thinks they're a tough guy and they're blowing off their mouth and then when something happens and you lay a little beating on them you're going to court for assault. He starts it, you finish it, and he takes you to court.

The VLTs are skinning people alive. I see it every day. People go to a club with $300, and when they leave they haven't got enough money in their pocket to get home. They're putting everything they got into the VLTs. You can't even go over and talk to them because the machine got them in a trance. Their eyes are bulged out. Their pupils are three times their normal size.

Some taxi drivers are hooked on them, big time. They'll come out at five or six o'clock in the morning. By the time twelve o'clock rolls around and they've made $200, they're gone then to sit in front of a machine. They'll be on the road then until six or seven o'clock in the evening trying to make a shift. If they can't they'll come to someone like me who owns his own car and say, "Any chance you can loan me a shift? I haven't got a drop of gas to put in the car." If you need to put a bit of bread on your table, I got no problem giving it to you. I'll give you the shirt off my back as long as I think you need it. But I'm not giving you 5 cents to help feed your habit. It doesn't work that way.

Last year, one of our drivers was going to beat me up. Me and him were on the same car. I worked days, and he worked nights. He was hooked on the VLTs. I'd get the car off him, check the gas and check the oil to make sure she was topped up. Just about every day she'd be down five, or six, or seven dollars' worth of gas and down a half-quarter of oil. That's coming out of my pocket. If I got to spend ten bucks a day, that's fifty bucks a week. That's $200 a month. That's over two grand a year.

Every morning I passed in the receipts and the boss would go to him for whatever it was he owed him. At the time, the car wasn't mine. The company owned it. Eventually, he got fed up and told the boss he was going to punch me in the mouth. "He's more than welcome to try," I said.

I was at Petro Canada on Topsail Road, and the manager said, "Frank, he's going to flatten you."

I wasn't leaving that alone. I walked over to his car and said, "Do you have a problem?"

"Yeah," he said. "You're an asshole."

"Everyone is entitled to their opinion," I said. "But you know about opinions. They're like assholes: everyone's got one, and they all stink."

"I'm going to punch you in the mouth," he said.

"Before you do that, my son, let me give you a piece of advice. If it doesn't work out to your advantage, you're going to be one sorry son of a bitch. Let's get that straight before this goes any further. Are you still ready to rumble?"

"Oh, yes," he said.

He got out of the cab, and I bet the shit out of him right there in the Petro Canada parking lot.

The next day, I got a call from the police. "This gentleman you had a fight with yesterday wants you charged with assault causing bodily harm. He's got a few nice marks on him."

I had to get a lawyer. "I'm not pleading guilty," I said. "I had a fight with him, yes, but he asked for it. Besides, the gas station got the whole thing on video."

In court, the judge said, "Sir, you want to be wary of who you associate with."

I said, "Listen, I know who I associate with, and I try my best to stay clear of them, but it just didn't work out that way. This is not like any other job. Sometimes you're put in situations you don't really want to be in, but which you can't get out of. You got to stand up for yourself and do what you do best."

I ended up with an unconditional discharge.

I talked to the prosecutor out by the courthouse. As luck would have it, me and him used to get on the beer together at the university. "You know, this isn't the only time this is going to happen. I'm a cab driver. The same people the police cart off on a Friday and Saturday night, some of them slip through the cracks, and I get them. I don't have a nine millimetre. I can call for backup, sure, but it might take ten or fifteen minutes before anyone gets there. By then I'd be dead on the sidewalk. I got to be the way I am in order to survive."

My wife has asked me when I'm going to stop fighting.

"When I get out of the taxiing racket," I told her.

Getting Set Up

Darryl, driving and dispatching for forty years

As I get older, I'm not so familiar with faces, which is kind of strange, which is kind of opposite. People usually remember faces, but I remember voices. I can be at the shop or at a bar, and I'll recognize the voice of the person talking behind me. *I know that voice, I know that voice.* Even now, years after I gave up dispatching, I can usually put a voice to an address, or a voice to a particular run. I might not remember what some drivers look like, even the ones I worked with for years, but I'll never forget a voice over the radio.

Wherever the dispatcher sent me, as soon as the customer said where they were going, I instantly recognized them. I knew who they were and what their morning routine was.

My voice might register with them then, too. "Do I know you?"

"I never drove you before, missus, but I'm sure I've taken your calls."

They were almost always glad to put a face to that voice.

Over twenty-five years, I learned to trust voices.

I picked up a guy downtown. "Where are you going, my buddy?" I asked.

"Take me to the Topsail Road entrance of Donovon's."

If you're any bit personable, you try to make some sort of small talk with your customer. You might start off with the weather, for instance, but by the time you get to where you're going you're probably after talking about politics and religion and everything in between. With this guy, I never got a gig.

I tried feeling him out: "Not a bad night."

Nothing. I couldn't get a thing out of him. It's pretty strange when someone doesn't have at least something to say to you, especially on a long trip like that.

One thing kept going through my mind: *I'm getting set up to be robbed.*

Nobody likes to get robbed, whether it's a $5 fare or a $50 fare, because whatever they get comes straight out of your own pocket. It's a double-whammy. You got to pay for the shift and then you never earned any money for that night. Even worse, you could get stabbed or beaten. Today, if you're going out over the highway you want to get paid up front. If the driver is cute about it he'll drop his money off at a secure location in town, like a gas station.

We were getting pretty close to where he wanted to get dropped off, and I saw the cops coming towards me on the opposite side of the road. At the time, I was driving a Crown Victoria, one of those old RCMP police packages. I flicked the headlights, and they pulled me in.

"Holy Jesus," I said. "The cops just pulled me in."

Still nothing out of him.

I got out and headed back to the cop car. "I don't know what's on the go with this customer," I explained. "He hasn't spoken to me since he got in the car. I think I'm getting set up."

One of the cops got out, talked to buddy and asked him for some identification. Everything seemed fine.

With them tailing us, I drove him to a kind of small nondescript office building. The parking lot was deserted. I never stuck around to see if he went in.

As I pulled out, I noticed the cops were stopped across the road, watching.

That customer might not have meant any harm, but something didn't feel right. I never thought too much of it afterwards, but I often wondered what would've happened if the cops had never shown up.

Just Out of Dorchester

Dave, driving for twenty-two years

They sent me on a call to a fairly decent area of town, a fairly decent neighbourhood. A guy came out with a bottle of rum in his hand. He had a big, long, red beard and, to me, looked like something out of a lumberjack camp.

I said, "Where are you going to?"

"Whitbourne."

I said, "Have you got the money?" You always look for the money up front.

He showed me he had a handful of twenties. He said, "Do you mind if I drink this bottle?"

"No, go right ahead."

On the way out, we had a little chat, and he said, "I just got out of jail in Dorchester. I did six years for manslaughter."

I thought, *Jesus, great!*

I pulled up in front of his house and there was a big party on the go inside. There were cars everywhere. I didn't know if it was a welcome home party for him, or what was on the go. By this time, he was asleep, and I had to wake him up. He looked around: "Where am I?"

"You're home. This is your house. This is where you told me to take you to."

He said, "What is on the go here?"

He ran out of the taxi and into the house. Honest to God, there were people jumping out of the windows. He was in there going mad; he was like a lunatic. I could hear pots and pans and glasses smashing.

"Jesus," I said, "I got to try to go in and get paid by this guy."

I went up and everybody was running out to their cars taking off. It was like a bomb had gone off in there. It was like something you'd see on *The Simpsons*. I knocked on the door and went in and looked around. He had his wife up in the corner like that. [*Makes a strangling motion.*] "You whore. You slut." He was screaming all kinds of old stuff.

"Buddy," I said, "you owe me eighty bucks."

"I'm not paying you."

I said, "Listen, man. You just got out of Dorchester doing time for manslaughter. I know you're on some kind of undertaking. You don't want me to get the cops. The police are only down the road."

And with that he made a run at me. Like I said, he was pretty drunk by this time, and there wasn't much to him. I just flipped him over my hip and got him to the floor. I said to missus, "Missus, come over. He's got money in that pocket there. Take out the eighty bucks he owes me, and I'll go get the police."

"Oh, no," she said. "We'll work it out."

A Sobeys Bag Full of Beer

Gordon, driving for eighteen years

There was a guy walking around downtown with a big beer gut and his shirt off. He had a trench knife, the kind with the brass knuckles on the handle. They're illegal. A customer I had in the back told me to watch out for him. Just as he said that, I drove by the guy, and he went up George Street towards Trapper John's. I thought to myself, *I got to see what this is all about.* When I got around to the back of Trapper John's, the police had him surrounded. Three guys were wiping blood off themselves with a T-shirt, and one of them had the tip of his nose cut off. His friends tried to help him, and they got slashed and cut and were bleeding all over the place.

Knives aren't uncommon. I've had knives pulled on me. It's funny because I teach knife fighting. About ten years ago, I had a butterfly knife. It was a Filipino Balisong. They sometimes call it a "Manila folder." I was practicing tricks while there was nothing doing, and I got a call. I picked up this young guy. "What would you do if somebody pulled a knife on you?" he said.

"What kind of knife?"

He reached into his jacket and pulled one out. It was a little switchblade kind of job.

"I'd just take this out," I said, took out my knife and started doing some tricks.

"Oh, that's a nice one." He put his knife back in his pocket, and any intention he had of robbing me was gone out the window.

But knives aren't the only thing I've had to contend with. About four years ago, I picked up three guys on Richmond Hill who were wasted on cocaine. This was about four o'clock in the morning.

They wouldn't give me a destination—just directions. Most cab drivers don't like that: it makes them uneasy. "Why don't you tell me where you're going?"

After a while, he said, "We're going straight now. We're done with the turns."

We went right up to Bay Bulls, and one of them started laughing. "We're going to rob you now."

I locked her up and jumped out. "Well, let's go. There's only three of you. I can handle that."

"Never mind him. He's an asshole," his buddy said.

One Friday night, I was in the car waiting for some guy for about ten minutes. This was just off Golf Avenue, there by Buckmaster Circle. I could hear him bawling at me from the steps: "You haven't got that cash register on have you?"

"No, but I've been waiting a while. How about getting in?"

"I'm going back in the house for a piss," he said.

"All right, if you're doing that, I'm going to have to turn the meter on."

He came down from the steps and started calling me every name under the sun.

"Listen," I said, "are you going somewhere? Where are you headed to?"

He had a Sobeys bag full of beer, five or six bottles of beer. "I got a good mind to smack you right in the conk," he said.

"If you think you can get away with it, be my guest."

So he hauled off with the bag of beer. I struck him with a right jab, and he lunged at me and tried to tear my ear off. I had all kinds of scratches on the side of my face, and there was blood. I grabbed him and lifted up his eyelid with my index finger and shoved my thumb against his eye. "That's what it's going to cost you," I said. As soon as I let go with my hands, he lunged at me again. I got him with an elbow and bounced his head off the windshield. Then his friend came out and tried to help him. He dove over him and pinned my hands beneath me. I tried to head-butt him and get my hands free. His buddy then took him by the hand: "Let's get out of here!"

"Yeah, get him out before I call the cops," I said.

"Go ahead," he said, "you call the cops. I saw it. You hit him first."

It was that or get the face cut off me with a bag of beer.

"Get your beer," his buddy said.

I knew what he was going to do. He faked like he was getting the beer and dove at me. I grabbed him by the hair and gave him another three quick ones. The next thing, about ten of them came running out of the house. I managed to get the car moving, but she wouldn't do much because the timing chain was broke. I coasted down over the hill—no brakes, no power steering—and got to Rickett's Road and radioed in: "Send me another cab and a tow truck."

My buddy picked me up. "He started the fight," I explained. "He hit me with a bag of beer. I was only defending myself. I gave him a few knocks and a whole slew of them came out of the house."

"The tow truck is coming," he said. "Where are you headed to now?"

"Take me back. I'm going to finish what they started."

"No, you can't do that."

"Yes, I can," I said. "Watch me. Drop me off on the sidewalk, and I'll take care of it."

"Think," he said. "There could be some person across the street looking and see you showing up and cleaning house, and you're the one who's going to get arrested."

And then I saw the logic of it.

But you'd be surprised what's out there: guns, knives and pepper spray. Gang beatings—that kind of stuff. At one point, there was a group of about twenty from Middle Cove going around. They had nearly beaten someone to death at the top of Solomon's Lane, just by The Ship.

I was driving east down Water Street heading towards George Street. It was about three o'clock, and a big fight had broken out. There were about thirty people trading punches. I had a little baton stick about that long [*He holds up his hands a foot apart.*] hidden under my leg. I could see a couple stood up in the doorway of Templeton's, the wallpaper and paint shop. The guy put his finger up to signal me. I stopped and buddy got in and slid across. His girlfriend was just about to get in, and this guy came over the bonnet, shoved her aside, reached in and grabbed buddy by the throat and hauled back to drill him. "Who do you think you're putting your finger up to?" he said.

He was one of these heroes. His buddies were into a fight, and he picked someone at random, a soft target, to look like a big shot. It's pretty easy when you got a guy in the back of a cab sitting down. I made a roar at him: "Get out, or I'll cave your skull in!"

He had his fists up and looked at me, saw the stick and just dropped the passenger and jumped out.

Missus was all shaking: "Who's that? Who's that?"

"I don't know—some nut," her boyfriend said. "Thanks for taking care of that, cabbie."

"No sweat. That happens every now and again."

Guys Like You in Prison

Frank, driving for twenty-nine years

I picked up a guy at the King's Bridge Hotel at about four o'clock in the morning. This was twenty years ago. He looked really pale, and he was shaking like he was in shock. I said, "Where are you headed to?"

"We got to wait for somebody else."

This other guy came out, and he had to be six-five. He was covered with tattoos. You could tell he just came from prison because he had that prison swagger about him. If you've ever been to prison, you'd know what I'm talking about. He treated the guy in front like dirt, and he had this girl with him. I kind of figured out that it was either buddy's sister or girlfriend or wife, and this guy was having his way with her in the back of the car. The guy was just too scared to say anything.

When she got in, she said, "Oh, we got a good-looking cab driver tonight."

Buddy started running his fingers through my hair. "Oh, yes," he said, "Isn't he sweet?"

I don't like guys like that. I had just seen this movie *Roadhouse*, and there was this line in the movie that I loved. I thought, *Now is my opportunity*.

"Give it up!" I said. "I used to fuck guys like you in prison."

Buddy's jaw dropped, and the colour drained out of his face. He couldn't believe I said it. It was just like I hit him with a shovel or something. I stunned him for about two minutes. The other guy, the little one, I thought he was going to have a stroke. He thought it was all over. And then buddy in back let out the big roar, the big belly laugh. He said, "You got some balls. No one gets away with saying stuff like that to me."

"No man gets away with running their fingers through my hair, either."

When he got out, he ended up giving me a $10 tip, plus the fare.

Level-Headed

Danny, driving for three years

I came down past the Sheridan Hotel, and there was a guy in a pile on the ground by this bar. His head was down, and I could see his body kind of jump trying to breathe. He was choking. Two big brutes were just stood there doing nothing. I stopped, and I said, "Why don't you roll him over so he can breathe?"

One guy said, "It's best for you to get the fuck out of here."

I said, "Is it worth a man dying on the street when all it takes is for you to roll him over?"

"He passed out. He had a seizure."

"I don't care what he had, man. Roll him over. He's going to choke." I then recognized one of them as a guy I used to work for. "Man, he's going to die, and the two of you are going to go to jail for the rest of your lives."

He knew I was a level-headed guy, and he rolled him over. You could see the body heaving up and down breathing. That poor guy was beat to fuck. His face was messed up like Quasimodo or something. They did a number on him. I don't know what happened, and I didn't pick him up. I called an ambulance to go get him.

I'm Not a Tough Person

Janet, driving for six years

For many women, the workplace is the site of violence, harassment and bullying. In 2004, over 350,000 work-related incidents of violence were reported by women. While the vast majority were physical and verbal abuse, 24 per cent were incidents of sexual assault. But this only accounts for a fraction of the total number. Assaults against women are consistently underreported. Statistics Canada has estimated that only 20 per cent of women who are the victim of violence bring it to the attention of police. While assaults by strangers account for only 15 per cent of the total number, working with unstable or volatile persons and having a mobile workplace are contributing risk factors.

I've always been a caregiver. Even growing up, I had a big family, and I helped take care of my brothers and sister. Then, of course, I had my own children, and I took care of them. I worked at the hospital and the CNIB. After I went through my divorce, I wanted to do something that didn't involve having to take care of somebody. I'd just had enough. I wanted freedom. You're in my car now. You could go to the corner store on Queen's Road. You're going to get out, and I don't have to worry about you anymore. That's the way I wanted things to be.

I always wanted to drive a taxi, but I didn't think I had enough knowledge of the city to do it. One morning, I just got up and said, "That's what I'm going to do."

It was fast-paced—hectic. You sort of got to be Johnny-on-the-spot. For the first three days, I had a tremendous headache. Then I said, "You know what? You can do this." I just relaxed, and then I loved it. I absolutely loved it. I come out here every morning, and I rarely miss a day. This year I missed two or three weeks because

I ended up with pneumonia. That's rare for me. But I work six days a week, and I love it.

You got to realize, there's 180 or more guys working at this stand, and four women. I never wanted to become one of the guys. I didn't want that. I wanted to keep my identity. That's not to say that I don't want somebody to open a door, or to pull out a chair for me. I just didn't want to be standing around, telling dirty jokes and spitting on the sidewalk. That type of thing. A couple of the guys here said that I wouldn't make it because I wasn't tough enough. I'm not a tough person. I don't have a tough exterior. But men get in my car, and they'll try to say and do things. They'll say things to see if they can get me going. Sometimes they'll make a grab for you. My best defence against that is to just ignore them. Recently, there were a couple of guys talking in the back seat. One of them said to me, "What's your favourite food?"

"Pasta."

"What's your favourite day of the week?"

"Probably Sunday."

"What's your favourite colour?"

"Black."

"I figured you'd go for black," he said. "A big black cock."

For the most part, the things they say are mostly sexual. It's really just dirty talk. The majority, I think, are in their early twenties. Some are university students. But I did have three Irishmen in the car who were with one of the oil companies, and they were saying they'd like to have a couple of women for the night. I didn't even listen to them. One started rubbing my shoulders and then he asked me if I had a daughter that they could rent. I found that very distasteful. I said, "I'm assuming you don't have daughters, or sisters." That sat him right back on his ass.

I've only once had a problem with violence. I picked up this guy and took him to where he wanted to go. He said he had to run into his sister's house and get some money. I waited four or five minutes. I tooted the horn, but he didn't come out. I could see him chatting with someone in the kitchen, and I knocked on the door. I said, "I just want to get paid. Give me my ten bucks, and we're good. I'll be gone out of your hair."

He got a little upset. He said, "I told you to wait in the car."

I thought, *This is not going to be good.*

He threatened me. He was going to kick the guts out of me. He was going to beat the car up. It was pretty scary stuff.

I called into the dispatcher and told him what was on the go. He sent the police, and the other drivers kept checking on me while I waited. By that time, the meter was after running up to $52. The guy was arrested, and he had to pay me back the money in instalments, $5 a month, through the court. The court wanted me to go down and write a victim impact statement. I said, "No, I wasted about two hours on this guy. That's more time gone out of my life than I care to waste on the likes of him." I heard later that he's very violent, and he was arrested just a couple of weeks ago and charged with beating up two women.

Going to War

Sandra, driving for four years

There's times when I'm going out and I feel like I should put on a helmet. There are times I feel like I'm going to war. There's been a few times when I've had to pull off to the side of the road. I think, *That's it. I'm not doing it no more.*

I had two guys in the car recently. One was sensible, supposedly. The other wasn't. He was absolutely loaded. Loaded or not, one of them could still manage to say, "Come into my house, and this is what I'll do to you. I'll do it to you better than anyone else has done it to you, and you don't have to do nothing."

How I address it is I sort of shrug it off: "No, give it up. That's enough now. Go in the house; I got to work."

The last going off, I just said, "Thanks, but no thanks."

You know that it's only going to be some kind of whacky deviant who is going to go out and rape some stranger. But you're down on

George Street, or you're picking up at a house, and you don't know where you're going with them, or you don't know what's waiting on the other end of the trip. You just get them where they're going and hope that it isn't a tangly long run. If I got myself into a situation where I felt unsafe I wouldn't hesitate to stall out the car on some main road and say, "Listen, I got to get you another cab."

It's mostly agitating, the sexual stuff. The other day, a guy and his three buddies used the word "pussy." And then they apologized for using it. I said, "No, I'm fine with that."

Then they went, "Oh, you're fine with that. So how's your landscaping going?"

And those were men coming from a big house. They were well educated and well dressed. There were no hoodies. There were no ball caps on sideways. They weren't old and drunk. Those are the most intimidating, the over-forty, educated, got a wife, a nice house and a good job. They'll look you right in the eye, and they're not drunk. That's the difference—they're not drunk.

One guy taught me a good lesson. It was Halloween, and he pointed to the meter and he said, "How much are you going to make in the next hour? Whatever it is, I'll double it. You just come into the house."

I said, "You're kidding, right?"

He looked me straight in the face and said, "Seriously, this is your last chance. I will not make this offer to you again."

I went, "You really should get out."

Now that was intimidating. He wasn't loaded. I won't say he was sober, but he wasn't loaded, and he had the nerve to say that to me.

If someone touched me in some way I didn't like, I could slam on the brake. He'd have no legs. He'd go right up over the seat and probably hit his head on the console. You can do that; that's an option. If someone grabs you the wrong way, if you got your seatbelt on, or even if you don't, you know you're doing it, so you can brace yourself. Slam on the brakes, and they throw themselves up onto the front seat. I slammed on the brakes a couple of times and just watched them go. And they do, they just fly like they're in an accident. Then they'll say something right accusatory: "What did you do that for?"

"Okay, you just asked me if I could give you a blowjob, repeatedly. I asked you to stop, and then you touched my arm. That's why I did it."

It happens, but it's not too common. Rarely do they touch your face. You don't get too many that touch your face, and you don't get too many that touch your neck. It's your shoulder, arms, and sometimes you'll get a hand on your leg. They rarely "accidentally" bump your boob.

I've heard things from men that I had to go home and look up on the Internet. These are things I don't want to know. It's so graphic, it's *porno*graphic.

You got to roll with the punches. What's the word I'm looking for? Maybe it's passive. How passive am I? What I thought was rolling with the punches, is that being passive?

One of my friends is completely traumatized by the raunchiness of it, the stuff we've all had said to us. But this person's background is so hardcore that I don't grasp why it's devastating her so much. She said, "What can I do? Can I use bear spray, or mace?"

I never carried anything in the car. I know people who have. I've gotten into taxis and there's a magnetized knife attached to the radio. I've heard of concrete being put into the bottoms of Pepsi bottles. One of the girls went to talk to the police about it. They said, "Use the mace and answer questions later." But you still got to answer questions later, and God forbid you end up whacking someone whose daddy got lots of money and can get them out of a jam.

You can't always cry for help, either. You got to make sure that when you are hollering out you need it. Like I said to my friend, "Make sure that if you're in a situation you're going to be ready to start calling out for help, you let someone know where you're at." Personally, I wouldn't call out unless I absolutely had to. But if she wants to spray people, maybe you should get another job.

Some drivers aren't much better than customers. I was single for a period of time. Every driver who will cheat on their wife will hit on you. Just like if you walked into a store every clerk who knows that you're single will hit on you. So they start crawling out of the woodwork. That's why when I go out to a club to have a few drinks or to a friend's house I don't want to be driven home by certain people. It just makes it uncomfortable the next day, especially when they think they can hit on you in the same dirtbag way that the customers do.

So, guess what? It's not just a customer thing, it's a male thing. I've had a few friends of mine who said, "We need a ride to a party. Come in and have a smoke." And I've done that. I've walked into parties—and I don't know if it's common—but they'll have porn on at the party. It's like background music. And no one is supposed to notice what's going on? I walked in and one of the guys sat down was a friend of mine's son. I go in and here he is sat down watching porn. And they think it's normal. It's one thing if it's a Friday night and you and your boyfriend are watching a bit of porn. But it's totally something else if you and your buddies are sat around getting drunk watching it at a party with a houseful of people.

When I said to a few cab drivers about the stuff that's being said to us, one of them just looked at me: "Do people really say that shit to you?"

People don't quite grasp it. They're thinking of what might be said but until they hear it themselves they sort of skirt around the reality of it. When I talk to my boyfriend about it, I'll talk around it, too. Like, I don't say to him, "Last night, some buddy tried to grab me by the boob."

With my boyfriend, I'm not verbally descriptive. He knows some of the stories because he's sat around when a bunch of us are all talking. But I don't think any of them get it. And with him it's weird. I don't see the same anger that I would project if it was my daughter, or if it was my wife, who came home after someone crowded her in a corner and said they were going to take her home and do this and that to them.

I can't help but think, *Why aren't you saying something? Why aren't you more concerned?*

One thing I refuse to do is deliveries after dark, and I won't bring in groceries after dark, either. We got a little old lady, and she gets so mad at me. But I don't care. She goes to the grocery store at three o'clock in the morning, and she wants the groceries brought in. We call her the "paper towel lady." She's OCD, so she buys a load of paper towels, and I guess she wipes down her walls with them, or something. I get her to the door, and then I leave.

That's the part that makes me nervous: being in parking lots in the dark. No, you don't do that. If you were walking home, you'd never cut through the parking lot of an apartment building. I don't want to have to do deliveries where you got to walk into the building at night and walk out again. That's one of the areas I'm scared of—alone in a parking lot at night. There are parties in apartment buildings where you might be bringing in beer and cigarettes. But then on the way out you could have a bunch of guys watching you. Then there's the other issue of me having money in the car, or having money on me. I don't want to get caught up in that crossfire.

You Can't Leave the Scene of an Accident

Danny, driving for three years

Taxi drivers are not just the victims of assault. They are also the victims of property damage both in and out of their cabs. They've been rear-ended, side-swiped and T-boned, while some—foot-heavy and frustrated—admitted to causing accidents. On any given Friday or Saturday night, the majority of taxicabs are going to or coming from the downtown area servicing hundreds of customers who are intoxicated. Some cabs—like when a customer is passed out and incommunicative—are put out of commission for hours. More than a few customers are dead drunk and vomit up over the back seat. Those cabs usually don't get back on the road until the next day.

I was coming down Torbay Road. There are four lanes, two lanes going south, and two lanes going north. I was in the left lane going south. Some guy was in the furthest lane going south with me, which is the northbound lane, doing eighty. I phoned into the police and reported him: "Buddy is loaded on the wrong side of the road."

A half an hour later, they called me back: "He's in his house. We need your statement to arrest him."

I said, "If he made it home, he made it home. What do you want me to do about it?"

"We need your statement to arrest him. You'll be the one pressing charges."

"I'm not doing that. He made it home, and no one was hurt. But I guarantee you he is a repeat drunk driver, and he's still at it."

It makes you not even want to phone in drunk drivers. Why phone them in when the police are doing nothing about it? I see them going up Hamilton Avenue all the time—that's one of the major arteries in the city. I'm doing sixty or sixty-five. I usually won't go twenty kilometres over the speed limit. That way the police don't bother with you. Then you got a drunk driver doing forty or fifty over the speed limit. It's the prime time of the night, and he's doing 100 kilometres an hour. He's obviously drunk. Drunks don't go nowhere near the speed limit, and they're swerving all over the road. What are you going to do, phone them in? Then you get interrogated by the police about who you are and what you're all about. Then that drunk will get into an accident or run someone down and you've got to deal with it. That shouldn't be.

Two years ago, my buddy, Danny, got into a bit of a fender-bender. The guy was driving an Acura sports car. It was one of the high-end models, like a Mercedes, not one of the ones you see around here. Buddy rear-ended Danny here in the Tim Horton's parking lot. I got out making sure Danny was okay, and I kind of positioned my car so buddy in the Acura couldn't take off. The guy had gone into Tim Horton's without even realizing he had rear-ended someone. He came out, got back in his car and blew the horn at me. "Move out of the way," he said.

"No, I'm not getting out of the way, man. You just rear-ended someone. You can't leave the scene of an accident."

He got out of his car and walked across to the Tim Horton's.

Me and Danny were talking. "Are you all right, or what?"

"Yes, but my neck is a little sore."

I called the ambulance.

"The ambulance will be here in a minute," I said. "They'll probably throw you on a stretcher."

Buddy came out with a coffee in his hand, a big black coffee. I knew right off the bat he was drunk. He was like, "What are you harassing me for?"

"What do you mean, harassing you?"

He said, "You blocked me in. You wouldn't let me leave. Do you know you can be charged for that?"

I'm like, "Hold on now, bud. You just rear-ended a guy. How come you're not asking him if he's okay? You're more worried about getting away. That tells me you're drunk. Are you drunk?"

With that, he turned around and went back into Tim Horton's for the third time.

The cops came and then the ambulance took Danny off. He had whiplash.

I told the cops that I didn't know for sure if buddy was drunk. It turned out later that he was a lawyer, a high-end lawyer, and that he was drunk. It was his second offence. I guess he was trying to throw a coffee in himself to sober up. I couldn't believe that someone so highly educated could be so stupid. I wouldn't care what was going on, if I was drunk or not. My priority would be to find out if anyone was hurt. That guy was obviously a straight-up pig. Where are people's morals?

Getting Sick in the Back Seat

Paul, driving and dispatching for seventeen years

Physical violence? No, but I've had people fighting over a cab.

Like if you got in on one side and someone else got in the other. Both doors are open, and you're arguing over who got in the cab first. I'll just drive down the road and whoever wants to get in can get in. I've had people throwing up. I would tell them, "If you get sick, you're cleaning my van. I'll haul into the gas station, and you're going to clean up the mess while the meter is running. If not, I'll get the cops, and they'll make you pay for it." The cops will make you pay $80 to have the van detailed.

One fellow threw up on the side of the car. Another one I took to Paradise, and when I got out by Smith's Home Furnishing, he got sick. He threw up right on the mat. I took the mat and all and just heaved it out onto the side of the road and left it. No mess anywhere else—that was it. I had four nurses heading home from downtown. When I turned off of Adelaide and onto New Gower, one of them got sick. When I got to Mount Pearl, she got sick again. I parked at North Atlantic Petroleum on Commonwealth and Brookfield, shut off the motor, and they went in and bought Pine-Sol, Windex, paper towels—the whole shot. When they got it cleaned up, the van smelled better than ever. They were nurses see, and they were used to that kind of stuff.

I explained to the wife, when I get you in the van and it's January or February, and I know you're drunk, I'll put down the four windows. I'll freeze you. You're more likely to throw up when you're warm, but not if you're froze to death.

Zombies
Danny, driving for three years
There are two types of zombies. There are zombies, and then there are kamikaze zombies. It's all got to do with the late hours of the night. There are the kamikazes that jump right in front of you. They don't care if you're moving at thirty, forty or fifty. They're coming out, and they're coming after you. They'll kill themselves right on the bonnet of your car for a ride home. Then there are the

zombies, like something out of *Night of the Living Dead*. You're coming down over the hill and their eyes and their mouths are hanging open. They're eating pizza, and they got it all down their shirt. Their eyes are crossed. They're screaming; their hands are reaching out.

I've often come in on Pitts Memorial Drive, and they're out the highway. When you're coming out on the highway you're about doing one-twenty. I've often come in doing 170, or 180. About two weeks ago, there was a kamikaze right on the fast lane walking out to Kilbride. I phoned the police: "There's no light there. He's going to get killed, and a cab driver is going to go to jail for it."

"We'll send out a cruiser. If he's still there we'll have a chat and let him be on his way."

As far as I know, you're not allowed to walk out a highway. You're not allowed to hitchhike, or anything. You got two cruisers sat there on George Street. Send one up, put him in the car and cart him off. Or call a cab and get him to pay for the run home. I know I'm not going to pick them up. That's a zombie right on the spot. That's the kind of crew we're picking up every weekend. You got to be careful. My son, you don't know what half of them are going to get on with when they get in the car.

I Never Heard Nothing Until I Got Into This

Fitz, driving for fifteen years

According to folklorist Hagar Salamon, when someone tells a myth he or she enters into a kind of cultural dialogue with the listener. Myths convey messages. They address and respond to the dilemmas of human existence, and their repetition provides belief that solutions exist. Myths are not just confined to "primitive" societies but are threaded through modern social life. They use symbols, or signs, to "enable their transmission in concentrated messages." Taxicab drivers often repeat "the myth of the naked women" as a means to mediate and to challenge the strains they experience in dealing with the public.

The myth is defined by symbols—race, gender and social status—which articulates their uneasy relationship with female customers.

I was a bartender for thirty years, but when they put the machines in I got fed up with it. I got fed up with it because there was no money to be made at it any more. Anyone could change tickets and ashtrays. Now they don't even need you to change ashtrays. I was getting kind of bored with it, anyhow. I thought, *Jesus, I got to get something else.* My buddy spoke to me about taxiing. Right from high school he was in the industry. He said, "Go in and get a licence and drive the car for me in the daytime."

I said, "Right on. It sounds like a plan."

My brother-in-law owned a stand. I said, "Do you have a car to give me, or what?"

"Sure," he said.

That's how I got at taxiing.

I've been working with people all my life. I thought I was after seeing it all and hearing it all at the bar racket. But I never heard nothing or seen nothing until I got at this.

One morning, I went over to Hatcher House at the university, and two little Asian people came out, a girl and a guy. They put their luggage aboard, we're going out over the road, and I happened to hear her giggle. I looked in the rear-view mirror, and here she had nothing on. I said, "What's on the go?" Buddy never even had on a pair of socks. They were trying to get in a little dart before they went on the plane back home.

People are unreal. They get in your car and they figure they own it: *You do what I tell you.* But they forget that there are other people who got to sit in the car, too. Many times, I'm after turning around and saying, "You can't be doing that. What do you think you're doing?" Then they look at you like you're crazy, or something. To them, you're only a dumb taxi driver, and I got to listen to what they're telling me. To a certain extent, you do have to grin and bear it. What else can you really do? But you get kind of used to it after a while.

They sent me up to Chancellor Park one morning. It's a place for elderly people who got to be watched around the clock. I went up and waited and waited. I called up the dispatcher: "There's no one coming out of here."

He said, "I'll keep you in mind. There's nothing doing, anyway."

Next thing, out comes missus. She had on a three-quarter length mink coat. [*He uses a French accent.*] "Take me to the hotel down by the water." That's what she said to me. Now there's a load of hotels down by the water.

"My darling," I said, "which one?"

"Drive."

I drove down and, sure enough, she was talking about the Newfoundland Hotel.

"Wait," she said and went in.

Exactly a half an hour went by: "Take me to that other hotel."

The Delta was what she was talking about.

The meter was still ticking away. I hauled up, and she went in. Another thirty minutes went by, and out she came and sat in the car: "Take me to the other one again." I went out the road, and I was talking away to her. She was saying where she was from, that in Montreal things were a lot faster. Then the next thing I know, she opens up her coat, and here she got not a tack on—nothing. Not a tack, not a tack. She said, "Do you want this, or do you want to get paid?"

I said, "My darling, I can get as much of that as I want home. [*He points to the meter.*] Tick, tick, tick."

She peeled off $400: "Thank you very much."

Dealing With Drunken Women

Danny, driving for three years

While it is illegal to deny someone access to goods and services based on gender, in a recent CBC article entitled "St. John's Taxis Leery of Young Women," one company spokesman indicated that because they feared accusations of sexual impropriety some drivers were leery of pick-

ing up young women. There was an immediate backlash from women's organizations. In a press release, the executive director of the Coalition Against Violence stated: "Negative ideas about young women exposed by this taxi company are incorrect and disrespectful." Doug McCarthy, president of Co-Op Taxi, was quick to point out that, in the past, drivers, protecting their livelihood and their safety, had always picked up women first, couples second and men last. "Now," he said, "that's reversed."

At first, my girlfriend was a little skeptical about me driving a cab. Her main concern was driving after four-thirty and having to deal with the drunken women, the Jabba the Huts. It's always the big, fat, nasty woman that'll say, "I'll show you my tits for a run home."

I'm in the car alone: "Ah, no." Maybe if it was Pamela Anderson, or something, I'd consider it.

I used to tell the girlfriend that she didn't have to worry about anything. "I'm out working. If I come home every Saturday night with $40, then you got a reason to worry. I'm gone for twelve hours, and I got next to nothing made. You can phone down to that stand to find out if I'm working, and they'll tell you." I got to punch in and out when I'm gone on a call. If you're not going to take a call, you let them know. If you want a break, or a coffee, or tea, or whatever, you let the dispatcher know. If you're messing around, you got to take your name off. It's only easy for the girlfriend to know if I'm up to no good.

They Don't Know They're in the Car

Michael, driving and dispatching for thirty-seven years

If a bartender comes out and puts you in my car and I haul away, it's my responsibility that you get home. I just can't put you on your doorstep and say, "I'll get the money tomorrow." Even if I get paid and drive off and leave you there you could tip over in the snowbank, or you could strike your head off the concrete. You could die right there on your doorstep.

When you pick up some of the younger crowd coming out of Liquid Ice at seven in the morning, they're gone—wrecked on ecstasy and cocaine. You name it, and they're on it. You might put them in the backseat, and they say they're going to Hayward Avenue. There's nobody going with them. They're in the car, but they don't know they're in the car. They don't know they're in the world. But they're going to Hayward Avenue. Once you put on that meter and drive away they're your responsibility. Once you get to Hayward Avenue, then what do you do?

You got to watch what you're doing, too. People come out: "Take so-and-so home." They put her in the car. She's eighteen, or twenty years old. She's a university student. It's probably her first time in town. It's probably her first time downtown. She's got a little dress on. She's drunk; she's stoned. You get her back to campus, and she may trip when you let her out. She may scratch her leg, or tear her dress. She may tear her slacks. She wakes up the next morning and phones the police, and you got to go explain all this old stuff. Once your name goes in the paper for anything like that, sexual assault, the thought will always be in the back of people's minds: *Did he do it? Was it him?* You may be innocent, but if your name ends up in the paper for sexual assault you got one hell of a job to try and clear yourself. You're the last one to have seen her. Between here and there you had no one else in that car but her. There was one driver who was charged and went to jail. It could easily happen out there now. When you bring them home, you just don't know.

You Get Fucked Over, and Nobody Gives a Fuck

Derrick, driving for eighteen years

Most crimes against taxicab drivers are petty theft. Sometimes they are what the Criminal Code defines as "common assault," which includes the use of force, both directly and indirectly, or threats. It is often the frequency and not the severity of these crimes that con-

tributes to the perception that little is being done by the police to pro-
tect the taxicab driver's safety and to catch perpetrators. Taxicab driv-
ers are left to swallow their fear and anxiety and get back behind the
wheel. But now they have a knife kept in their boot, or a sawed-off
hockey stick beneath their seat: "We got to protect what's ours."

Think about it. You can go into Walmart and rob a $4 shirt and you're prosecuted to the fullest extent of the law, to the point of going to jail. If you rip off a taxi driver for $50, it takes the cops over an hour to get to your location, and then they have the gall to say, "What do you want me to do about it?"

"I want him arrested, and I wanted him prosecuted. That's your job. He didn't pay me. I want my money, or let's get him arrested."

I had two kids arrested up in Foxtrap after taking me for a milk run. They owed me sixty bucks. I said to them, "I'm going to get you." And I caught them. But this is what the goddamned courts did. Without giving me sufficient notice to show up and plead my case, they convicted one of them and told him to pay me. I never saw that money. With the other kid, at least they notified me in time. I went down to the court, and the prosecutor comes over: "Blah, blah, blah. He's in school. He's a nice kid."

He paid me my thirty bucks, his half of the fare. I didn't get the second half of the fare. What's wrong with that picture? I get ripped off, and he gets a smack on the wrist.

Another night, I had two kids going to Kelligrews of all places, which was another $60 ride. The last kid gets out and gives me all these coins wrapped up in dollar bills. There's a $10 bill, and inside that $10 bill are two coupons. And they're supposed to be two $20 bills. Here I am with a $60 ride, and I all got for it was $18. My employer doesn't give two fucks about you ripping me off. He sees me with those kilometres, and I got to give him so much money. It's an industry where you get fucked over, and you get fucked over, and nobody gives a fuck. Do you understand?

Doing the Cops a Favour

Dave, driving for twenty-two years

Taxi drivers have a working relationship with the police. Come two o'clock in the morning cars are flying left, right and centre. Cab drivers don't drive slowly. Most times, if you're passing police they'll flick their lights for you to slow down. Some of the rookie cops will pull you over and give you a bunch of tickets. But they don't understand that we're actually doing them a favour. I've often pulled up on the back of Rob Roy on Duckworth Street, and there'll be a riot going on. I'll open my two doors and say, "Come on, boys. Get in. If you don't come with me you're going down to the drunk tank until Monday."

I was only at it two months and a cop gave me a load of tickets on Adelaide Street, George Street and Church Hill. All in one shot—one whole load of tickets. Someone must've called and complained about some of us using Adelaide. I passed by twice that night and never thought anything of it. That's what I thought the cop pulled me over for. I had a customer in the car, too—a drunk.

The cop said, "I got you for a signal light and two rolling stops."

The customer said everything to him. He called him a no-good bastard and a fucker. "This guy's out here trying to make a good living, and you're giving him a hard time."

The cop listened for a little while and then threatened to put him down in the drunk tank. That shut him up.

I gave the customer a run home for free.

I took the ticket to court. I never bothered with my own representative because I couldn't afford one. The Crown attorney was like, "What do you want to do?"

"I just want the fine reduced, and I don't want any points." The cop was a nice guy. I said, "I know you picked me up for those rolling stops and the signal light, but we do you guys a favour hauling the drunks away. Sometimes we can't come to a complete stop. We got to sneak around cars to get out from around George Street. If we stop, we hold up the lane."

"I know," he said. "But we had to do what we had to do."

The Crown agreed to half the fines and no points. But it went on my record. I ended up paying $250.

Cab drivers are out all hours of the night, and we like to keep an eye out. Up off Stavanger Drive, I saw a guy on a pedal bike dressed all in black with a knapsack on his back. He was creeping around the neighbourhood. I phoned the police: "I just wanted to give you a heads-up, a tip."

You know, they were more concerned about who I was and what I was doing than what that guy was up to. Can you believe that?

Another time, my kid's best friend's pedal bike got stolen. I was sat in the car and watched some guy ride right past me on it. I was looking straight at the bike—it's an $1,800 pedal bike. It's not cheap. I phoned the police and said, "My kid's best friend's bike was recently stolen. I don't know if it was reported stolen or not. But I just saw it go across the street right in front of me."

They said, "Who are you? Where are you from? What's your name? We can't take you at your word that that bike was stolen, unless it is reported."

"I'm telling you that bike is stolen. I know that bike. I did the brake lines on it myself, and there are tire wraps on it. I put them on. It had fluid brakes in it. I had to turn them off because they weren't working right."

I gave them all the information so they could phone me back and let me know what they were going to do about it. I watched buddy go right by two cops. I thought, *What the hell is going on?*

Finally, I called the police back. "The guy went right by two police officers."

They ended up doing nothing.

I know they got their hands full, but when people are reaching out for help or asking for assistance they should help them. Don't ignore the call or investigate the person who is calling.

They got that guy on Craigmillar Avenue who was breaking into houses. He had over 12,000 material items. Who's to say it wasn't the same guy on the bike dressed all in black? I used to do a little bit of robbing when I was younger. That's how you do it. If someone goes out late at night wearing dark cloths, a knapsack and got no identifying marks, it's a dead giveaway. That person's not going to work four in the morning.

I was coming up Monkstown Road on a Thursday night. A girl jumped out onto Monkstown Road trying to run away from her boyfriend. I slammed on the brakes, and I just missed her heels. If it had been a Friday night I would be in jail now because I would've been going twenty kilometres faster, and I would have nailed her. She was screaming in the most frantic voice you could ever imagine: "Help me, help me! Call the police!" Meanwhile, her boyfriend stopped, and there was another guy with him.

I told her to get in the car. I hauled out my cellphone, and held it up so buddy could see it. "That's the police; they're on the way."

I don't want to beat a guy up, or get beat up. I could get stabbed, or I could lose my life.

When she got in the car, her boyfriend ran over and kicked the door. I gave him a shove, and then he took off. I looked back at the girl. Here she had a shiner on her face.

Her friend was just there by Bannerman Park in a parked car. "Stop, stop, stop," she said. "That's my friend." She just jumped out and went on.

Where were the police when she was getting the guts beat out of her? They're walking up and down George Street talking to the girls—that's where. There are chicks hanging out of the two cruisers, tits and legs hanging out of the cruiser. What kind of message does that send? It sends a bullshit message, that's what it sends.

A People Person
Leonard, driving for four years

I like the people. I'm a people person, buddy. Yes, sir. I'm a 100 per cent people person. If you're not, you shouldn't be in this industry.

I get people in the car that I drive regularly. They have ADD. They want to go from point A to point B. They want to make sure you stop at every stop sign. They want to make sure you make a left when you're supposed to make a left and a right when you're supposed to make a right. If there's not exactly $5 on that meter, buddy, they go right off the deep end. When I get those people in the car, I don't turn on the meter. They say, "You never turned on the meter! How much is it?"

They're afraid you're going to say, "$5.25."

"How much did you pay last time?"

"$5."

"Well, $5 is fine."

I had a person in the car years ago. I got him down by Adelaide Street; he was stood up around a lot of people. They were intoxicated, basically. He looked like he was intoxicated, but he didn't fit in with the bunch stood up. People were waving and stuff, and I saw him. I knew he stood out for a reason. I picked him up and dropped him off at St. Clare's. I knew there was something wrong. I knew he wasn't drunk because he didn't fit in with the rest of them. I can't explain it to you. I just knew that. He ended up being a severe diabetic and almost died. Some guys will recognize that, and some guys won't.

Just to give you an idea. Do you remember that autistic kid that got arrested by the cops a few years ago? He was walking up Pennywell Road. Whatever way he was walking, the cops thought he was drunk, or something. They went over and confronted him. He was autistic; the cops were foreign to him. Whoever arrested him, and there were several involved, just couldn't get it. The cops didn't know, didn't care, had no training, or couldn't recognize that this young guy had some issues. They must've grown up under a turnip. Those people have no life experience, those young cops. We give them a gun and a badge and they start going around arresting people.

Hotheaded

Francis, driving for two years

You can't be confrontational with customers. That's what I've learned. When I first started, I ended up quitting three times because I was confrontational. You get people screaming in your face: "You do what I tell you to do, you dirty maggot." Stuff like that. I had four older brothers. The way I grew up was if someone gives it, you got to give back twice as hard—no matter what. Do you know what I'm saying? So driving a cab was a little bit of an adjustment for me. I ended up doing a few courses at MUN, philosophy courses. It chilled me out quite out a bit. But if you're not good in stressful situations and you're unable to problem solve or to negotiate then driving a cab is not the job for you.

I dropped my buddy off at a wedding up in Shea Heights. Him and his girlfriend are regulars. I noticed there were two cop cars and two supervisor vehicles in the parking lot. I pulled in and said to the police officers, "Do you need a hand with anything? Do you want me to take someone out of here?"

"Sure, no sweat." They turned around and started talking to a couple and some other guy: "Your best bet is getting in that cab and going home out of it."

I ended up driving them from Shea Heights to St. Phillips. One of them was after getting into a racket with a nineteen-year-old. He himself was a forty-odd-year-old. I call people like him "repeaters." They keep saying the same thing over and over and over again. Right from Shea Heights to St. Phillips, he kept saying, "Would you let anyone say anything like that to your wife or kid? Would you let anyone say anything like that to your wife or kid? I'll beat his head in; I'll kill him. I'll beat his head in; I'll kill him." He just kept saying it over and over again.

The guy in front was a local businessman—I knew who he was. He was just rolling his eyes and shaking his head.

Buddy in back then started classifying everyone from Shea Heights as scumbags.

His wife said, "Shut up out of it! Shut your mouth! That cab driver might be from Shea Heights."

I started laughing.

Buddy in the front asked, "Where are you from, cabbie?"

"Shea Heights."

The repeater said, "Where are you from, cabbie?"

"Shea Heights."

"You're just saying that now because I said everyone from Shea Heights is scum. They're all a bunch of scumbags up there, aren't they, cabbie?"

"I suppose. They're all scumbags." You got to agree and have fun with them. What are you going to do, disagree with them? You're not going to get anywhere very fast with that type of attitude.

You got to understand that there are people like that. I mean, he never directly insulted me. He never said, "*You're* a scumbag cab driver." He was just generalizing. It just so happened that he got into a racket up in Shea Heights. It could've been Paradise, Torbay—anywhere. Even then, you can turn around and tell him to shut his mouth. But that's only going to lead to more nonsense. The best thing is to take your cellphone, dial the police and show him the number. That usually takes care of everything.

That same weekend, I could've had another altercation. We don't like to pick up groups of guys. They're too much trouble, especially if they're buddies. There's strength in numbers. When you come down over Queen's Road you look for couples. You don't want to be picking up three or four guys. You can pick up a bunch in suits, and it'll be the same thing. Just because they're in suits doesn't mean you're not going to get trouble. I passed a group of four guys, and this girl was stood out on the corner. I stopped, and she said, "Come on!" She's what we call a "baiter." She stands up and gets a cab to stop, and the guys get in.

They got in the cab, and I said, "Where are you headed?"

"Empire Avenue."

There's four different Empire Avenues. You got the one by the Taxation Centre, and you got the one by Columbus Drive. That breaks off and goes up by Mundy Pond and Blackmarsh Road. Then there's one down by the stadium. I knew they were headed up by the crosstown, but I didn't know which side. I said, "Can you be a bit more specific about where the house is to? Can you name anything around it?"

The guy in the back said, "It's Tucker's Superette. Come on, dumbass. You don't know where Tucker's Superette is? Do you know what I'm saying, dumbass?"

I looked in the mirror and as I made eye contact with him he looked away. I don't take personal insults. I'm pretty easygoing; I get along with everybody. But I don't take personal insults.

One Friday night, a driver radioed in and said that he needed help on Kenna's Hill. It's just down by the stadium. I stopped, and another of our cars stopped. Then a Newfound Cab stopped, and then a City Wide and a Jiffy stopped. Cab drivers help each other out. Remember that old guy that got that real bad beating? He ended up in critical condition. He was smashed up, and he was just an old guy. Some people have no bones about it. They don't care if you're young or old. We got to look out for each other.

Our driver was stood up outside with four young guys. To be honest, I don't know how to take this guy. He's had a bit of a history with altercations. A few times, he even drove people to the RNC building and got them arrested. He's a hothead, but he's harmless. What ended up happening was two of the customers were arguing and were about to get into a fistfight in his van. So he stopped the van and told them to get out. We were all stood up in the parking lot, and he was screaming, "I want my $10!"

The Newfound guy said, "Boys, it's either pay the $10 or you're going to jail, and you'll be in jail until Monday morning."

At this point, an undercover cop came along. She saw the ruckus, jumped out and flashed the badge. The boys paid the ten bucks.

I was walking to my car, and another car pulled up. There were four of them inside, big brutish, grizzly bears. They were screaming, "Get the fuck off the road! You cab drivers are all a bunch of scumbags."

They were obviously impaired, and they were driving. I tried to ignore them, and one guy said, "Get off the road, you fucker."

I said, "My car is off the road."

"Well, then, get them off the road."

"That's none of my business," I said. "Go around."

Then he jumped out and started walking towards me and pointing his finger: "I'm going to rip your head off!"

"You can go right ahead, but there's a cop right there."

As soon as I said that he went right into the ruckus.

I jumped in the cab, and then the three guys that were into the first altercation ran over to my car: "Any chance for a ride home?"

I was like, "Boys, are you serious? You were just giving that other driver a hard time, and now you want a run home?"

"We don't want to walk. It was his fault. We got a story to tell, too."

"Give me twenty-five bucks, and I'll give you a run. I'm not messing around."

"No sweat."

They paid the twenty-five right off the bat.

On the way, they got to telling me that here they were just carrying on with each other, and the driver thought they were serious. When I drove them, you couldn't have asked for any better. They were hugging me and patting me on the shoulder. To them, I was the best thing since sliced bread.

You got people beating up your car and slamming your doors. How are you supposed to deal with them? Get out and punch them in the head? Then you're on charges. We had a guy who got out after some teenager, and now he's up on charges. The teenager was throwing snowballs at the cars, and the driver got out. The teenager came over and made a swing. The driver is a boxer and made short work of him. The teenager saw the car number and the company name, and his parents phoned the police, pressed charges and took him to court. He's looking at honorary discharge and two years' probation.

He told me last week, "The judge asked me if I had my time back would you do it all over again? I would do it over again. If anyone makes a swing at me, I'm swinging back. Straight up self-defence."

The judge said, "It didn't occur to you to run? Why didn't you run away? Why didn't you call the cops and press charges?"

I know plenty of drivers like that. But that only leads to trouble. You got to feel people out. If you're hotheaded it's not going to work. For a good while, I was like that. I'm back at it full-time now, though, and I'm doing okay. But the major adjustment was with me.

Violence is Not the Answer

Bazil, driving for twelve years

It's getting to the point where someone is seriously going to get hurt for stiffing a taxi driver. It happens so much that the frustration level is growing and growing and growing. The taxi drivers are going to say, "We're fed up with getting beat up, picked on, used and abused. We're coming to our buddies' rescue." Now maybe these guys will never rip off a taxi driver again because they know what's going to happen to them. Guaranteed that's going to happen. Guaranteed.

It's quicker for me to get a couple of my buddies to come by and beat the shit out of you than it is to get the cops. And sooner or later, that's what's going to happen. The cops aren't going to get there in time and someone is going to end up in the hospital with a serious injury, or someone is going to end up dead.

Violence is not the answer, but it's getting to the point where something's got to be done to tell people to stop fucking around with the taxi drivers. You can't be ripping us off. Someone is seriously going to get hurt. Some taxi driver is going to haul out a baseball bat and beat the fuck out of someone. Internal injuries, broken legs. I can see it happening. But taxi drivers got to remember one thing—that if you take it out you better be prepared to use it. If you don't, they're going to use it on you instead. That's why I don't carry weapons. You're better off talking your way out of it.

Epilogue

Y Y Y Y Y Y Y Y Y Y Y Y Y Y Y

Honesty is the Road to Poverty

Theodore, driving for thirty-eight years
The neighbourhood stands are practically gone; they were gobbled up by the fleets. Some were sold wholesale, while others died a slow death. Some taxicab drivers might call this progress, or the inevitable consequence of increased professionalization, while others would say not much has improved and that the industry has lost much of its personality.

According to this driver, the stand owner he drove for didn't keep up with modernization—marketing and the pursuit of lucrative contracts which lure and retain brokers, the backbone of today's taxicab industry. An earlier monologue was more scathing in its reproach: "The owner didn't care. He was half-cracked. They never had a psychiatric assessment done on him, but he wasn't all there."

I was thirteen when I bought my first car. I quit school and bought a 1961 Valiant for $31. My mother nearly killed me with the heel of her shoe. I'll never forget it. I've had dozens of cars since then, but you never forget the first one. One night, I picked up two girls, and I had to push it down past the stadium because it wouldn't start. There was smoke going everywhere. You never had to have insurance, but you were supposed to have a licence. I didn't care. Most of the cops walked the beat, and you'd never haul in for them. They'd be waving their flashlights and we'd just go on. The car you were driving could be in some buddy's name from four owners ago. You can't get away with none of that now. Those were the good old days, buddy.

When I first started taxiing it was for Will Snow on Pearce Avenue. It was called Snow's Taxi. That was in 1973, I think. He probably had five or six cars, him and his brother, Jim. The dispatch was in behind his house in a shed. They used to call him "Dollar Will" because he used to drive his regulars for a dollar: "Give us a dollar. Give us a dollar." I wasn't allowed to charge you $2 if you were one of his regulars: "Well, Will only charges me a dollar." I didn't know the difference.

I worked down to Burgess Brothers' Cabs when old Jim Burgess was on the go down on the east end of Duckworth Street. That's going back thirty-five years. Jim Burgess was a well-dressed man and right proper. I used to clean their cars for 50 cents, and then I'd hop in a taxi to go to work. Burgess Brothers' Cabs was a good stand. They never did anything out of the way down there. There was no bootlegging—nothing like that. Certainly drugs weren't heard tell of. But I remember Crown Taxi on Springdale Street used to bootleg right on the side of the road. Buddy had a box that was as big as an outhouse. He had it stood up alongside a pole all the while when I was a kid. He used to bootleg from it. He didn't care if he drove a passenger or not so long as he sold a few bottles of liquor. The liquor store was just right there on the corner. When they closed, he'd open.

I was only with Burgess Brothers' Cabs a few months. At the time, I used to shift around a lot. If there was nothing doing at one stand I'd go to another.

I had my own taxi at Churchill Park Cabs which later became Golden Cabs. It was a 1972 Grand Marquis. It was beautiful; it was like a big ship. I'm telling you, buddy, you could sit eight people in there—four in the front and four in the back. Having my own car I found that I didn't want to work. I was better off working for someone else because then I was committed to it. When I had my own car, a young guy—single—I was gone. I didn't work half the time because I didn't need to. If I wanted a few dollars I'd sign back in. I was into work for a few hours to make a few bucks, and then I was gone again. But when I got married and had youngsters, I went at it, and I stayed at it.

I was with one stand for twelve years. They were up in centre city—that general area. They had a little stand there for years. I could've left there and went to a better stand. But I liked the people, and I liked the area. Sometimes, it's not all about the money. If you're content, that's where you stay. I was happy, and I did all right.

That area has got a hard name, but I never got into any trouble up around there. That kind of stuff wasn't heard tell of thirty years ago. I'll tell you why. I knew the crowd from Cashin Avenue and all the boys from the blocks. I grew up with them, and then I went taxiing with them. Sure, I lived on Cashin Avenue for eighteen years. I'd end up driving that crowd downtown, or to a party, and then they'd phone to pick them up and bring them back. I can't say I had any trouble with violence. That was never a problem for me. Not with that crowd, anyhow. I had to kick a guy out one night, a young guy, who was going to Shea Heights. He was best kind when I picked him up in Kilbride. When I got halfway out to Shea Heights he went cracked. He had a beer in his hand, but I didn't mind that. The next thing, he was going to hit me in the head with it. I hauled the car in, and I gave him one good kick out the door. I didn't care if he had to be killed. You can't let them walk over you. Forget that.

When I first started at my last stand they had twenty-seven cars, and when I left they only had four. They never went after the business; they never went after the contracts. The stand owner had an opportunity to buy Jiffy Cabs when Jiffy Cabs were nobodies, and he passed it up. He should've done it, but he wasn't into it enough, I don't think. He wasn't going cracked making a whole lot of money. Now he made good money, and he was happy with what he had. Going back thirty years ago, there were guys waiting two years to get on with that stand. That was the stand to be on. That was the money-maker. When they were really busy there weren't a whole lot of taxi stands around that area. That was the stand to be on if you could get on there.

The stand owner did a lot for people, too. He was a good guy. He did a lot for drivers over the years, and then a lot of drivers stabbed him in the back. They were getting their cars repaired and getting loans off of him—stuff like that. They never ever paid him back. He never told me, but I heard it a number of times. Drivers that drove with him for years, the older guys, will tell you the same thing. Now he wasn't an angel, either.

They've been into the bootlegging for years. It's to the point where if you ask a random person on the street where to get a bottle at three in the morning they'll probably say this stand. Here's a case in point. We had three men come in five-thirty one morning who wanted a bottle. I was just getting ready to go home. The dispatcher said, "No, we don't sell nothing here like that."

"Reach under the counter, give me the bottle, and here's your thirty bucks."

Then you would get the call when people are on the go at all hours of the morning to pick up cigarettes, mix and ice—different things. They want it delivered to such and such a spot. That happened a lot on weekends. But a lot of taxis are basically the same.

If you can get talking to a real honest taxi driver out there, he shouldn't be at it. He'll never make anything. He won't make any money if he's on the up-and-up. You might get an older man, a retiree, who just wants something to do part-time. You might find a few like that who want to get out of the house. Honesty is the road to poverty. You got to hustle every dollar you can off the meter. My son, that's the name of the game.

The last going off, the stand owner only had two cars. But he got no overhead. He got his operator's licence, he got his taxi licence, and he got a cellphone. Say, for instance, there's four of us here sitting at the table. I got the cellphone because I'm next out, and then I get a call. If you're next out, you get the phone. Then you pass the phone onto the next driver. There's no dispatcher, and there's no stand.

It's just too bad that the stand owner had to let it go down that far. He could've had it all—for sure.

I heard he recently got into an accident. I wasn't talking to him, but I heard he got into an accident one Friday coming down over Hamilton Avenue. He smashed up the car with three women aboard. Two of them got injured. Apparently, he was going too fast. He has been known to speed. He can get from here down to your house in three or four minutes. He's one of those. He doesn't care about speeding tickets; he was always like it. But this time he hit a pole or the back of another car, or something along those lines.

Now there's only one car down there. The guy who owns that must be there twenty-five years. One time, he used to work day and night. But not so much anymore.

I haven't taxied now in about five years. I got fed up with it; I got poisoned with it. You got to live in the car to make a dollar. I was up to the stand one night—it was pissing rain out—and all the boys were lined up waiting on a run. It was the middle of the week, and there was nothing doing. This guy came in off the street soaking wet. He wanted to go to Placentia. I couldn't say anything because there were three drivers ahead of me. I had to wait for them to refuse the run before I could take it. It ended up that no one wanted to take him. I went out to Placentia and dropped him off in the pouring rain. I never had a problem, and he gave me $125. When I came back to the stand, one of the drivers was still there waiting on a run.

I took on a regular job, and the wife worked at the time, too. I was missing everything taxiing because I was working weekends. On Fridays, I'd drive the truck, get a shower and then hop in the taxi until six o'clock Saturday morning. I'd go home and sleep, but you never really sleep. You're up again at eleven o'clock. You're back in the taxi then at three o'clock until Sunday morning. By that time, you're just about worn out. You're not fit to look at. I was crooked because I wasn't getting enough sleep. I did that for a few years, but then the wife said, "Look, you got to give that up." And so I did.

I can't say I'll never go back taxiing because I might have to do it tomorrow. Never say never when you're talking about taxiing. What you make is no amount, but it's enough to keep you going from day to day. But the thing about taxiing is you always got a dollar in your pocket. Taxiing is a job when you can't get a job. If all else fails, you can always hop behind the wheel of a taxi and go to work.

A Note on Sources

■▼▲▼▲▼▲▼▲▼▲▼▲▼▲■

Historian Graham Hodges wrote, "Taxis and cabdrivers are as ubiquitous in print and visual materials as they are in the streets." The sheer volume of popular literature documenting their experiences is, to some extent, overwhelming. But very little has ever been written on the St. John's taxicab industry. The life they lead has always had a curious fascination for the public. It seemed obvious, then, that an unbiased look at their working lives was necessary and long overdue. *The Other Side of Midnight: Taxicab Stories* relied on thirty-eight interviews conducted with St. John's taxicab drivers as its main source of information. This book took more than three years to complete; it could have taken much longer. One of the problems was the matter of degree and scope. In selecting critical details about the taxicab industry and the lives of its workers, other aspects were brushed over, such as the stand owners and the role of the suburban taxis, those taxis licensed in municipalities adjacent to St. John's.

Several monographs provided historical context and a general understanding of how urban taxicab industries operate. *Taxi: Urban Economies and the Social and Transport Impacts of the Taxicab* by James Cooper and Ray Mundy described the development of control and "the conflicts between those that wish to further regulate and those who wish to deregulate." *Taxi: A Social History of the New York City Cabdriver* by Graham Hodges brought together news reports, films and the writings of taxicab drivers to create a history of the community taxicab drivers compose.

The St. John's City Archives contained a sizable trove of primary sources painting a clear picture of an industry in a constant state of turmoil culminating in the 1989 Commission of Inquiry. The Commission's final report was vital, providing a comprehensive overview of the city's role as the industry's regulator. From studying the city's archives, it's clear that, by the end of WWII, the city had begun a more systematic approach to licensing and bylaw enforcement. The earliest complete list of St. John's taxi stands dates from 1951 when the number of taxi stands peaked. RNC Certificates of Conduct, memorandums between the city clerk and the taxicab inspector, and taxi commission meeting minutes are common throughout the files. There are even handwritten notes from one former taxi inspector detailing the process of licensing as well as extensive lists of unlicensed drivers the city wanted "rounded up."

The Centre for Newfoundland Studies and the Provincial Archives are relatively silent on taxicabs. But it was at the CNS where "Cab Fares and Regulations for the City of St. John's" was located. While the city began regulating the taxicab industry at about the turn of the century, this regulation, passed in September 1912, the predecessor to the Taxi Bylaw, appears to be the earliest known to still exist. Other files, like "Agreement with Hotel Taxi Drivers," included daily expense sheets invaluable in determining the social makeup of the drivers and their clientele. Mainstream news reports from the two local newspapers, *The Evening Telegram* and *The Daily News*, provided accurate descriptions of wartime and post-war working conditions. Under the Magistrates Court section of *The Evening Telegram*, a number of assaults against taxi drivers were reported. We know about these cases because some drivers took their fares to court to get paid.

The Other Side of Midnight: Taxicab Stories set out to understand St. John's taxicab drivers. This book presents some rare opportunities to travel some very odd roads. Taxicab drivers are neither saints nor swindlers. They are ordinary men and women who, in the routine of their daily working lives, often experience extraordinary things. If this book has made them more human, then it has succeeded.

Acknowledgements

Over the course of more than three years, I interviewed approximately forty taxicab drivers. They were open and generous to a stranger with a microphone who wanted to know about their daily triumphs, trivialities and indignities. One driver was the type of informant non-fiction writers and documentarians hope for but which are a rarity. He availed himself to multiple interviews and introduced me to his friends and co-workers. Thank you, sir. You're the finest kind.

For their constant love and inspiration: my partner, Lesley, and our beautiful daughter, Anja. Without my parents and in-laws, Frank and Marie, the road getting here might've been a rocky one.

Creative Books has shown me unwavering support and patience. Thank you Donna Francis and Pamela Dooley. And Todd Manning and Amy Fitzpatrick, for making my words look sharp.

A writer is only as good as his editors. My friend and colleague, Joan Sullivan, and Ed Kavanagh helped transform the manuscript. Joan deserves special thanks. Through working together on her theatrical adaptation of *Rig: An Oral History of the Ocean Ranger Disaster*, Joan, as well as the cast and crew, instilled in me a confidence that helped bring this book to its conclusion.

The Other Side of Midnight: Taxicab Stories would not have been possible without the hard work and dedication of a number of talented artists.

Darren Whalen designed the graphics. Thanks for always being there.

Wanda Nolan's conversations with a female taxicab driver provided vital observations.

Photographers Jared Reid, Steve Payne, Seamus Heffernan and Jacob White made these taxicab stories far more accessible.

Gerard Collins' keen insight and practical advice made me a better writer.

A lot of people were helpful and encouraging: Joel Thomas Hynes, Ron Hynes, Craig Francis Power, Keith Collier, Katrina Rice, Lorraine Endicott, Jason Conway, Helen Miller, Robin McGrath, Morgan Murray, Christopher Martin, Kerri Cull, Paul Collins, Ryan Cleary, Mary Power and Emily Gushue.

Many organizations also offered support: Newfoundland and Labrador Arts Council, Helen Creighton Folklore Society, CBC, Writers' Alliance of Newfoundland and Labrador, City of St. John's Arts Grants Council, *Our Times*, *This Magazine*, *The Telegram*, Centre for Newfoundland Studies, Eastern Edge Gallery, The Rooms and the Arts and Culture Centre.